sona
BOOKS

**First published in the UK 2022 by Sona Books
an imprint of Danann Media Publishing Ltd.**

© 2022 Danann Media Publishing Limited

Copy Editor for Danann Tom O'Neill

CAT NO: **SON0539**
ISBN: **978-1-912918-99-7**

Made in EU.

World Cup

L E G E N D S

Once every four years, the greatest players and teams from around the globe come together in a celebration of the beautiful game. Packed with colour, excitement, passion and drama, the World Cup has the world glued to their televisions as the biggest names in football dazzle and wow on the ultimate stage. From Pelé and Maradona to Ronaldo and Moore, some of the most iconic names in the history of football are synonymous with the World Cup.

In this book you'll find a host of fascinating features on the aforementioned legends, as well as the Magnificent Magyars of the 1950s and the best side never to win the World Cup – the Cruyff-inspired Dutch team of the 1970s. We also bring you the 50 greatest players to grace the tournament and take you on a journey back through some of the World Cup's most memorable moments – both good and bad. Enjoy!

CONTENTS

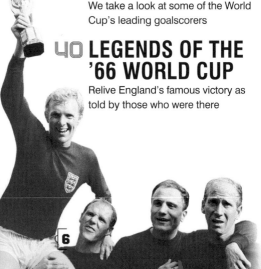

"ZIDANE SAW RED AND PAVED THE WAY FOR ITALY"

50 GREATEST WORLD CUP PLAYERS

Hundreds of players have appeared at the World Cup since it began way back in 1930, but over the past 21 tournaments some have stood out more than others

One of the most exciting things about the World Cup is seeing some of the globe's very best footballers strut their stuff on the biggest stage of all. It's a joy to watch footballers in their prime perform to the best of their ability, and while the most skilful teams don't always win, talent generally finds a way to shine.

To that end, we have players with sublime skill, and others who are so solid in defence that almost nothing will get past them. If anything, it's a disappointment that we didn't get to see all of the greats; had George Best, Alfredo Di Stéfano, George Weah and Ryan Giggs played in the tournament, for instance, they would certainly have made the list.

But that's not to say our top 50 is in any way anaemic; chances are any one of these players would make it into any team the world has ever assembled, club or country. All have shown brilliance or made their mark on the World Cup in ways that will always stick in the mind, and as such, we present them here in no particular order.

LIONEL MESSI

01 The feat of winning the World Cup has so far eluded Messi and his nemesis, Portugal's Cristiano Ronaldo. But Messi has arguably earned his place here by virtue of being the finest player during the 2014 tournament in Brazil. He was on the losing team in the final, but bagged four man-of-the-match awards and won the Golden Ball.

► Arguably the modern game's greatest player, Messi is yet to win a World Cup

CARLOS ALBERTO TORRES

02 Regarded as one of football's finest defenders, Carlos Alberto missed out in 1966 but captained Brazil in the final of the 1970 World Cup. A pass by Pelé in the 86th minute gifted him the golden opportunity to hammer home the fourth and final goal against Italy. It's still considered one of the best goals ever scored in the tournament.

ROGER MILLA

04 Roger Milla retired from international football in 1987, having made his first World Cup appearance for Cameroon five years earlier. But he came out of retirement aged 38 in 1990, scoring four World Cup goals and enthralling fans with his corner flag dance. He played again in 1994, becoming the oldest goalscorer at 42 when he put one past Russia.

ROBERTO CARLOS

03 A mainstay of the Brazilian team going into three World Cups, Carlos's skill at left-back helped his team reach the final in 1998. But while they lost against France 3-0, the number six emerged victorious four years later. All in all, he ended up playing an impressive 17 World Cup matches.

PAUL BREITNER

05 Breitner made 14 appearances for West Germany and scored four goals over two tournaments. None of these were more important than the 25th minute penalty to equalise against the Netherlands in Munich in 1974, paving the way for eventual victory and West Germany's second World Cup. He also scored in the final of 1982, but on this occasion ended up on the losing side, as Italy defeated West Germany 3-1.

LEV YASHIN

06 It's no surprise to see Soviet Union goalkeeper Yashin appear on the official 2018 Russia World Cup poster. His dominance between the sticks saw him shout instructions at his defence and collect crosses off the line in a manner that was unique at the time. He ended up playing 12 times in four World Cups, keeping four clean sheets.

LILIAN THURAM

07 The defender only scored twice for France, but what important goals they were. Finding his team 1-0 down against Croatia in the 1998 semi-final, he equalised within a minute before bagging the winner in the 70th minute. He went on to become a world champion, adding a European Championship two years later.

KARL-HEINZ RUMMENIGGE

08 Although Rummenigge lost two finals – in 1982 and 1986 – the winger was impressive in both tournaments. He scored a hat-trick against Chile in the 1982 group stages, and grabbed a goal in the 1986 final as West Germany attempted to get back into the game against Argentina. He scored nine World Cup goals in 19 appearances.

Rummenigge scored 45 goals in 95 appearances for West Germany

GIUSEPPE MEAZZA

09 The Italian national team, blessed with prolific goalscorer Meazza's talents, won two consecutive World Cups. Nicknamed 'Il Genio' ('The Genius'), he scored the only goal against Spain in the 1934 quarter final en route to victory (subsequently being named the tournament's best player), and he captained Italy to a 4-2 win over Hungary in 1938.

GORDON BANKS

10 As one of the best goalkeepers to grace a football field, Banks played in every game for England during the 1966 World Cup. Emerging victorious, he would prepare for games by chewing gum, spitting on his hands and smoothing them over. He could then lick his palms to make them sticky as opposition players headed his way.

OLIVER KAHN

11 Even though Kahn was named in the Germany World Cup squads in both 1994 and 1998, he only became the first-choice goalkeeper in 2002. By keeping five clean sheets and only letting in three goals (two in the final against Brazil), he was awarded the Golden Ball – the only goalkeeper ever to have achieved this feat to date.

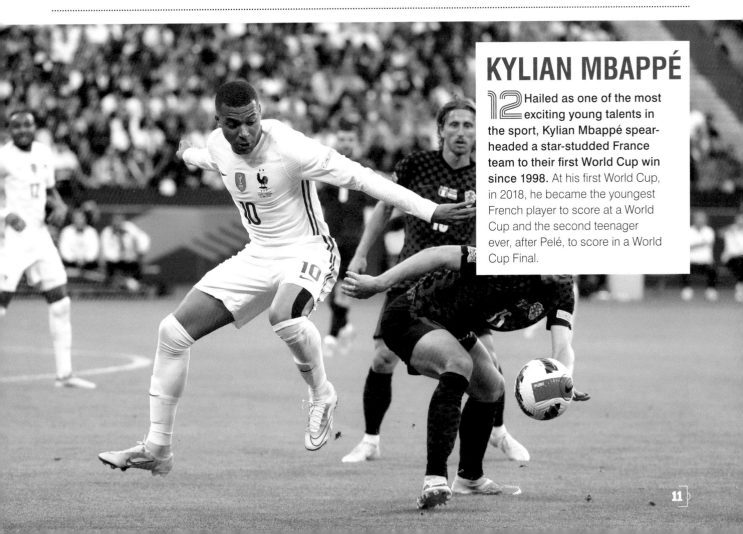

KYLIAN MBAPPÉ

12 Hailed as one of the most exciting young talents in the sport, Kylian Mbappé spearheaded a star-studded France team to their first World Cup win since 1998. At his first World Cup, in 2018, he became the youngest French player to score at a World Cup and the second teenager ever, after Pelé, to score in a World Cup Final.

GIANLUIGI BUFFON

13 With 175 caps, goalkeeper Buffon has not only played more games for Italy than any other footballer; he has appeared in five World Cup tournaments (1998, 2002, 2006, 2010 and 2014, playing in the latter four). His finest was the winning year of 2006, setting a record for conceding just two goals in seven matches with five clean sheets.

DANIEL PASSARELLA

14 Passarella is considered to be Argentina's greatest defender, but he could also score lots of **goals.** Calm and collected, he captained the 1978 winning team and, although he missed the tournament due to illness, he was named for 1986, making him the only Argentinian to be in both of the country's winning squads.

○ Baresi was one of the greatest defenders in world football

FRANCO BARESI

15 Defender Baresi won the 1982 tournament with Italy, and while he came third in 1990, he was **named in the FIFA World Cup All-Star Team.** He became captain in 1994, but despite missing a penalty in a final Brazil won, simply being there was surprising considering that he underwent surgery to his knee just three weeks before.

Klose holds the record for the most goals scored at World Cup finals

MIROSLAV KLOSE

16 **When striker Klose retired from international football on 11 August 2014, he did so a very happy player.** After all, just months before, Germany had won the World Cup for the first time since 1990. Klose had also scored in the 7-1 drubbing of Brazil in the semi-final, which saw him become the World Cup's all-time top scorer with 16 goals, just edging Ronaldo. That was his record-breaking fourth World Cup semi, and the goal (in addition to the one he scored against Ghana) put clear daylight between him and Gerd Müller as Klose became Germany's top goalscorer.

FERENC PUSKÁS

17 **Hungary's influential captain Puskás was easily the best player in the 1954 World Cup.** He was also part of one of the greatest sides the tournament has ever seen. As a talented inside left, this stocky player would practise his ball skills by juggling with a tennis ball, and his amazing shooting prowess was on display in the very first game. He scored two of the nine goals against South Korea, and helped Hungary to the final. But despite Puskás opening the scoring, they were beaten 3-2 by West Germany. Still, the man they called the Galloping Major due to his role in Hungary's army epitomised the 'Mighty Magyars, and his thunderous left foot will never be forgotten.

Zidane was France's hero in the 1998 final, but was dramatically sent off in the 2006 final against Italy

ZINEDINE ZIDANE

18 **Zidane won the World Cup with France in 1998, and he was certainly no bit-part player.** He scored twice in the 3-0 final defeat of Brazil in front of a home crowd at the Parc des Princes in Paris, and while they were his only goals, it added the World Cup to one of the most enviable honours lists in football. What set him apart was his composure with the ball and his knack of being able to pierce defences at the right moment. His passing was impeccable and his passing and dribbling crisp. The World Cup victory saw his face projected on the Arc de Triomphe.

LUKA MODRIĆ

19 Despite moderate success at the highest international level, Luka Modrić has led an underappreciated Croatian team to their highest placing since 1998. Modrić made his full international debut for Croatia in March 2006 in a 3-2 win against Argentina. In a disappointing international run, from 2006 to 2014 they failed to make it out of the group stage, and even failed to qualify for the World Cup altogether in 2010. However, in 2018 their fortunes changed, when Modrić led the team to a World Cup final matchup against France, with notable extra time wins against Denmark, Russia, and England in the knockout stages. They eventually faltered at the last hurdle with a 4-2 loss to France in the final, but their performance throughout the tournament is certainly one to remember.

FRANZ BECKENBAUER

20 Pelé was full of praise for Beckenbauer, famed for his stylish defending and ability as captain of West Germany. He influenced the nation both on and off the pitch as his country secured the World Cup in 1974, and winning the World Cup in 1990 as manager.

GARY LINEKER

21 Lineker knew how to find the net. As England's most successful World Cup striker with ten goals to his name, his clinical approach to the game saw him shoot six past opponents in the 1986 tournament (winning him the Golden Boot) and grab a further four in 1990. Three of those goals came in a blistering first-half hat-trick against Poland in the final group game of 1986, and it only cemented the reputation of a player known not only as 'Mister Nice Guy', but as a footballer with pace and an uncanny ability to find space in front of goal.

Zoff made his Italy debut in 1968 and went on win 112 caps for his country

DINO ZOFF

22 Zoff was aged 40 and 133 days when he lifted the World Cup trophy for Italy on 11 July 1982 against West Germany – the oldest player to win the tournament. As Italy's first-choice goalkeeper and captain during that summer, he kept two clean sheets and made a jaw-dropping reaction save in the second round against Brazil, ensuring his team preserved their 3-2 lead and progressed. Zoff was named in the All-Star team, and he was heralded as 1982's best goalkeeper. He also appeared in the previous three World Cups, keeping three clean sheets in 1978 as Italy came fourth.

RONALDINHO

23 Starring alongside Ronaldo and Rivaldo, Ronaldinho was part of a fearsome trinity that seemed almost destined to win Brazil the World Cup in 2002. His curling free kick from 40 yards in the quarter-final saw England's David Seaman floundering as the ball floated into the top-left corner of the goal. But he will also be remembered for the joy he seemed to get from football and the freedom he appeared to have with the ball at his feet. Able to instantly change pace and pass without a glance, he back-passed and step-overed his way to glory.

ROBERTO BAGGIO

24 In the USA in 1994, Baggio had the tournament of his life, and it earned him the Silver Ball as the second best player. The forward was undoubtedly Italy's top dog, scoring five goals and helping his country reach the final. This, however, is when Baggio's shine dimmed. After a 0-0 draw with Brazil after extra time, the game went to penalties.

Baggio needed to score to keep Italy in with a chance, but he put the decisive kick high over the bar and into the crowd, leaving him distraught and Brazil champions. Even so, he also scored in the 1990 and 1998 tournaments, making him the only Italian to bag goals in three World Cup tournaments.

Cannavaro was one of a long line of world-class Italian defenders

FABIO CANNAVARO

25 As captain, acclaimed defender Cannavaro led Italy to victory in the 2006 World Cup final, impressing fans by providing an almost impenetrable solidness at the back (Italy let in just two goals during the tournament). His strength, positional sense, awareness and timing earned him the nickname 'Il Muro di Berlino' ('the Berlin Wall') and this highly athletic player, who was as good in the air as he was on the ground, even went on to become the FIFA World Player of the Year; the first defender to win the award. All in all, this tenacious player made 18 appearances over four World Cups.

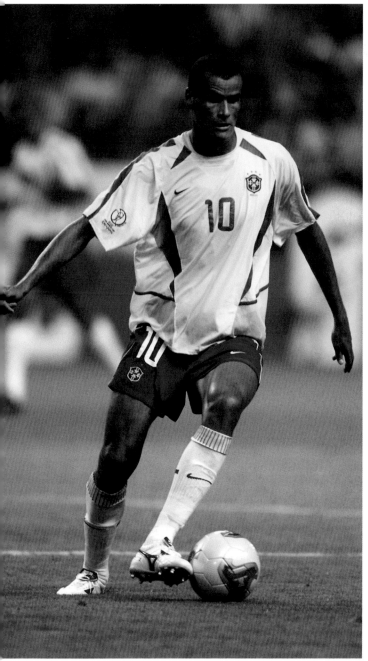

MARIO ZAGALLO

27 Winning the World Cup twice as a player (in 1958 and 1962) is always a triumph, but **doing so twice as a manager and assistant manager is something else.** To that end, left-winger Zagallo is about as ingrained in Brazil's success over the years as anyone could be, and he deserves the accolades he receives, even though some said he was fortunate to be playing. On the pitch, he was well-known for his runs from deep and his versatility. He also displayed tenacity and a never-say-die spirit. Favouring tireless hard work as well as style, he scored in that 1958 5-2 defeat of Sweden.

JOHAN NEESKENS

28 The Dutchman was a fantastic tackler and a **dead ball specialist.** He took part in two World Cup campaigns, with the Netherlands cruelly losing out in the finals of both 1974 and 1978.

RIVALDO

26 Think of Rivaldo, and you immediately conjure up images of his bending free kicks, tricky **feints and intricate dribbling.** You may also think about that match against Turkey in 2002 when the ball hit his arm and he fell to the floor clutching his face – earning opponent Hakan Ünsal a red card. Cheating aside, there is no doubting Rivaldo's skill, and it ultimately helped earn him and his Brazil team a World Cup victory that year.

GEOFF HURST

29 Hurst had only debuted for England against West Germany on 23 February 1966 – just months before the World Cup began – and he only gained a place in England's starting World Cup line-up in the quarter-final against Argentina after Jimmy Greaves became injured. He scored in that game and went on to set up a goal for Bobby Charlton in the semis, and impressed manager Alf Ramsey so much that he was given a place in the final. Hurst repaid the faith by cancelling out Helmut Haller's opening goal, but the game ultimately went into extra time. Hurst struck twice more to win the day.

Hurst made his name with a hat-trick in the 1966 World Cup final against West Germany

MARIO KEMPES

30 Argentina's explosive attacker scored two against the Netherlands in the 1978 World Cup final, which not only eased them to victory, but saw him end the tournament as both the top goalscorer (with six) and the best player. Those who watched him play would agree that his shot was devastating, and his calmness under pressure most noticeable. Yet he was also far from unassuming, playing with panache and becoming instantly noticeable for his personal style as well as his fast, on-pitch touches. For Argentinians he was a national hero, although the country crashed out in the second round of 1982 – a tournament that saw the introduction of Diego Maradona.

ZICO

31 Referred to as the 'white Pelé', Zico was a creative attacking midfielder whose eye for goal and technical skill were put to particularly good use in 1982. His goals helped Brazil win against Scotland, New Zealand and Argentina, so it was a shame for him that his country did not progress further than the second round.

In some ways it was a disappointment perhaps only matched by his goal in the opening match of the 1978 World Cup being ruled out. Still, such was his worth, Brazil worked hard to get him fit after a serious knee injury in 1986. In that tournament, he came on as a second-half substitute in the quarter-final against France. Unfortunately, he missed a penalty, and Brazil crashed out to France. There was no faulting his prodigious work ethic, however.

HARRY KANE

32 Harry Kane made his international debut in March 2015 at Wembley Stadium, scoring a header just 80 seconds after he was subbed on, in a win against Lithuania. Three years later, he was named captain of the 23-man England squad for the 2018 FIFA World Cup. In the group stages, he scored both of England's goals against Tunisia, as well as a hat-trick in the very next game in a 6-1 win against Panama; this was England's largest ever World Cup victory. Kane became only the third England player to score a hat-trick in a World Cup match. England finished a disappointing fourth after losing to Belgium in the third-place playoff, but Kane earned the Golden Boot as the top goalscorer of the 2018 World Cup with 6 goals.

CAFU

34 **His country's most capped footballer with 142 appearances, and it's easy to see why.** An amazing full-back, Cafu could burst down the right side of the pitch, essentially becoming an attacking right-winger. When Jorginho was injured in the 1994 final, manager Carlos Alberto Parreira had no worries putting Cafu in to replace him, even though he'd only made two appearances as a sub prior.

By the time 1998 rolled around, Cafu was a firmly established international. Brazil were beaten in the final, but they had better luck in 2002 when, as captain, Cafu led them to a 2-0 victory over Germany. During that tournament he was relentless, firing past opponents en route to the trophy.

GERD MÜLLER

33 **Nicknamed 'Bomber der Nation' – or 'the Nation's Bomber' – West German striker Müller scored 14 goals in the two World Cups in which he appeared (1970 and 1974).** He quickly became an icon for winning the 1974 World Cup with a decisive goal in the 43rd minute against the Netherlands. Just as memorable was his winning goal in the quarter-final of 1970 against then-world champions England, who were 2-0 up after 49 minutes. West Germany fought back to draw level before Müller struck the winner in extra time.

He would startle opponents with a rapid burst of pace over a short distance, and would throw his short body into the air above taller players to accurately head a ball. Many an opposing footballer could only watch as he turned tightly with great balance, yet he was also humble and reserved even in victory.

GARRINCHA

35 **Manuel Francisco dos Santos, to give his full name, won the World Cup twice – in 1958 and 1962 – but it was the later tournament that made his name.**

He stepped in for the injured Pelé and rose to the occasion, so much so that he was named the best player in 1962 and became joint top goalscorer.

Garrincha's strength was his strong control of the ball, amazing dribbling and powerful shooting. He was especially good with free kicks and corners, and he'd relish toying with opponents, not being afraid to show them up by displaying his talent to the max.

Gazza bursts into tears as England are beaten by West Germany in the 1990 semi-final

PAUL GASCOIGNE

36

Most remember Gascoigne – or Gazza – for the semi-final in 1990 when he earned himself a yellow card for a foul on West Germany's Thomas Berthold and promptly broke down in tears knowing that he'd be unable to play in the final. In the event, England didn't make it that far, but the memory sticks, as does the feeling that such a great talent should have graced more than six games at a solitary World Cup.

Why? Simply because Gazza was one of England's great talents. A flawed creative genius, he played as an attacking midfielder and his passing accuracy was superb, as was his protective skills on the ball, not to mention his great pace and strength. It's really unfortunate that his off-field activities clouded a great talent, but for many England fans he helped define 1990. If it wasn't for his assist to Mark Wright to get the winner against Egypt, England may never have got out of the group stage.

PAOLO ROSSI

37

Rossi's preparation for the 1982 World Cup had been far from ideal. He had just returned from a two-year ban for his involvement in the 1980 betting scandal, Totonero, which found many Italian football players guilty of match-fixing, and he had only been on the pitch for three games.

Manager Enzo Bearzot wanted him, however, and so the number 20 started in the opening stalemate against Poland. He came into his own during the second stage, scoring a hat-trick against Brazil. He then got two against Poland in the semis and opened the scoring in the final as Italy beat West Germany 3-1.

All was forgiven (although Rossi always denied being involved in match-fixing), and Bearzot's decision to choose and then stick with him paid off handsomely. But then Rossi was always intelligent, agile and prolific, and what he lacked in strength he made up for with incisive finishing and positional sense. His six goals in 1982 earned him the Golden Boot.

MICHEL PLATINI

38

The French side of the 1980s was strong, and this was in great part down to the attacking midfielder Platini. The team had learned their lessons from 1978 when they were knocked out at the group stage. Although they only scraped through the groups in 1982, Platini got on the scoresheet against Kuwait and

scored again against West Germany in the semis, eventually losing on penalties.

Platini was known to be one of the finest passers of the ball. He was also a prolific goalscorer, and he went on to lead France through the 1986 groups, before scoring against Italy in the round of 16 and Brazil in the quarters, a game they won on penalties.

BOBBY CHARLTON

39 With his trademark combover blowing in the wind and his name famous the world over, the Busby Babe who survived the Munich air crash in 1958 and established himself in Matt Busby's Manchester United was a key player for England during the three tournaments in which he was selected (he didn't kick a ball in 1958, but starred in 1962, 1966 and 1970).

Of those, 1966 was the most memorable for obvious reasons. He opened the scoring against Mexico in the group stage, and got two against Portugal in the semis. Most of all, though, crowds loved his thunderbolt shooting, which he could perform with either foot, and they adored his simple yet confident dribbling and the passionate elegance with which he played. As arguably the most gifted English football player in the team, he carried himself with a sense of gentlemanliness, earning the respect of both his fellow players and rivals.

○ Charlton was a key part of Alf Ramsey's World Cup-winning team in 1966

Eusébio wowed the crowds during the 1966 World Cup in England

TEÓFILO CUBILLAS

41 Born in Lima, Peru in 1949, Teófilo Cubillas is a Peruvian footballer who seemed destined for a career in football from the very start. In his first season, aged just 16, he was top scorer in the Peruvian Primera Division in 1966, a feat he repeated in 1970 as well. He was characterised as an attacking midfielder renowned for his exquisite technique, alongside fearsome shooting and free kick taking abilities. Featuring in three World Cups (1970, 1978 & 1982), Cubillas was selected as Peru's greatest ever player and is considered by many as the maximum reference for Peruvian football. He is also the midfielder with the largest amount of World Cup goals (with 10) and an astonishing 0.77 goal average.

EUSÉBIO

40 England may have won the World Cup in 1966, but Eusébio won hearts across the world. Playing for Portugal, he was awarded the Golden Boot for his nine goals while showcasing superb dribbling skills, athleticism and speed.

Famed for his right foot and nicknamed 'the Black Panther', 1966 turned out to be Eusébio's only World Cup, and he certainly made the most of it. When Portugal fell behind by three goals against North Korea, he fought hard to score in the 27th, 43rd, 56th and 59th minutes, putting his country ahead before José Augusto de Almeida grabbed the fifth.

There was an uneasy feeling that he would do the same to England in the semi-final when he got a penalty in the 82nd minute to make it 2-1. He didn't. Instead, Portugal got knocked out, but Eusébio opened the scoring in a 2-1 defeat of the Soviet Union to give Portugal their best-ever placing of third.

JAIRZINHO

42 So many Brazilian players from 1970 deserve to be named footballing icons, but none of them scored in every match that summer – except for Jairzinho, that is. He scored against Czechoslovakia, England and Romania in the group stages, grabbed the final goal against Peru in the quarters, helped Brazil to a 3-1 win in the semis, and popped up in the 71st minute of the final against Italy. He could have had two against England, if not for a crucial interception by Bobby Moore.

Jairzinho's performances earned the forward the nickname 'The Hurricane', and crowds rarely failed to gasp when he got up speed and pumped a lethal shot into the net. What's more, his success came despite him breaking his right leg twice.

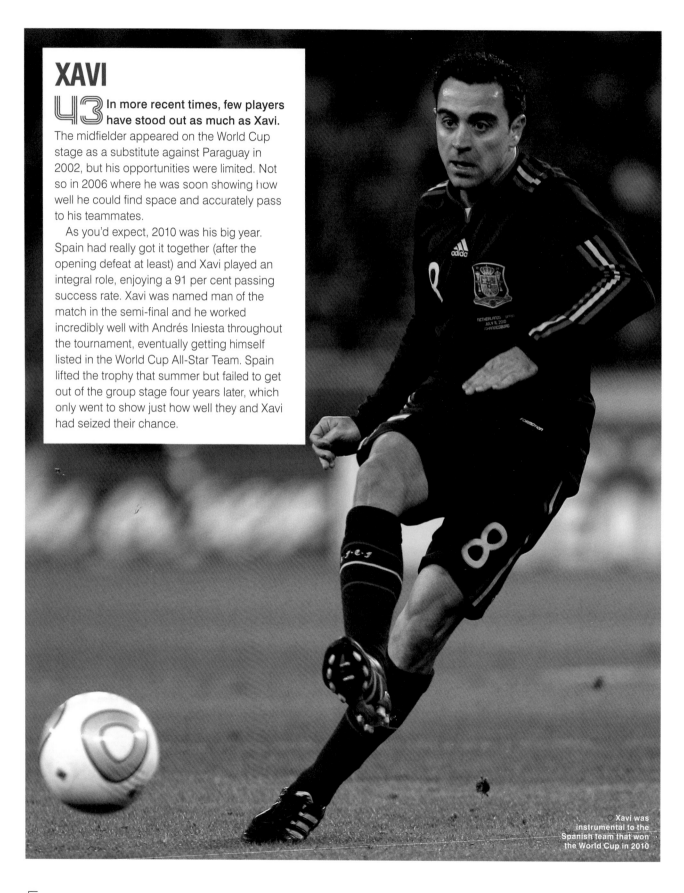

XAVI

43

In more recent times, few players have stood out as much as Xavi. The midfielder appeared on the World Cup stage as a substitute against Paraguay in 2002, but his opportunities were limited. Not so in 2006 where he was soon showing how well he could find space and accurately pass to his teammates.

As you'd expect, 2010 was his big year. Spain had really got it together (after the opening defeat at least) and Xavi played an integral role, enjoying a 91 per cent passing success rate. Xavi was named man of the match in the semi-final and he worked incredibly well with Andrés Iniesta throughout the tournament, eventually getting himself listed in the World Cup All-Star Team. Spain lifted the trophy that summer but failed to get out of the group stage four years later, which only went to show just how well they and Xavi had seized their chance.

○ Xavi was instrumental to the Spanish team that won the World Cup in 2010

ROMÁRIO

44 Romário's first World Cup in 1990 was a bit of disappointment, but then he had just recovered from a broken leg, and he wasn't fully fit. He only played for 65 minutes during that tournament before coming off for Müller in the match against Scotland. Far more impressive was 1994, however, when Romário made the World Cup his own.

A falling out with coach Carlos Alberto Parreira almost meant Romário didn't go to the USA that year. Only a furore back home saw him recalled to help get Brazil through a knife-edge qualifier. It was a wise decision, and one Parreira would never regret. As USA '94 got underway, Romário scored five goals and led Brazil to a fourth World Cup, displaying impressive ball control and an effectiveness at cutting past defenders. His skills rightfully earned him the Golden Ball for being the best player of the tournament.

JUST FONTAINE

45 Fontaine set a high standard when he lit up the World Cup of 1958, scoring a mammoth 13 goals – a record that stands to this day. Making it even more remarkable is the fact it was achieved over six matches, so he was off to a flying start before the group stage was out.

He continued his streak into the quarter-finals with two goals against Northern Ireland. But although he scored against France in the semis, they were knocked out by Brazil, so Fontaine's efforts only saw his team earn third place. As a striker, however, there were few of equal, which makes it all the more sad that he never played another World Cup – injury forced him to retire in 1962.

PELÉ

46 Edson Arantes do Nascimento is, to many minds, the greatest footballer to grace the World Cup. Playing in four tournaments, he made his debut in 1958 aged 17, and he competed in 1962, 1966 and, most notably, in 1970.

A prolific goalscorer, he had lightning pace and immense poise. He played with grace and could accurately shoot with great power on both feet. Unlike some talents, he worked with his teammates rather than as an individual. He was stylish and efficient: goalkeepers had little chance when he rolled up to take a penalty.

It is no surprise, then, that he holds the record for the most World Cup wins. His first tournament saw him score one against Wales in the quarter finals, three versus France in the semis and two in the final against Sweden. While he was injured for most of 1962 and persistently fouled through 1966, he accepted a call-up in 1970, playing six games and scoring six goals. Pelé really was the complete player.

Maradona's goal against England in 1986 is one of the best in World Cup history

DIEGO MARADONA

47 Ask any England fan to name a famous moment in World Cup football, and a good number will point to the quarter-final against Argentina in 1986. Having displayed his incredible brilliance, he found himself heading towards goal, slipping past England's Glenn Hoddle with ease. His pass hit the foot of England's Steve Hodge, sending it towards the penalty area, at which point Maradona pounced – and hit it with his outside left hand. It thereafter became known as the 'Hand of God', but Argentina's captain Maradona was more than just that moment.

When Maradona had the ball, crowds would lick their lips with anticipation. With his physical strength, close ball control and jaw-dropping dribbling skills, he was able to score five goals in 1986 and make five further assists. In doing so, he helped Argentina win the tournament that year before putting in another glorious set of displays four years later when he was named Italia '90's third best player. So while he marred his reputation by being sent home in 1994 for testing positive for ephedrine, there was a sense that his job was done, and his legendary status secured, making his nickname 'El Pibe de Oro' ('The Golden Boy') very apt.

RONALDO

48 With 15 goals over 19 matches, Ronaldo was, until 2014, the World Cup's top goalscorer. But while he has since been pipped by Miroslav Klose, he will always be one of the greatest icons of the tournament.

He first appeared in 1998, when he scored four and was named the best player as Brazil were pipped by France. It set Brazil up nicely for 2002, however, when they won courtesy of two Ronaldo goals against Germany.

Yet that doesn't actually tell the full story. Prior to the 2002 finals, he had been out of the game for 15 months after rupturing the cruciate ligament in his right knee. That caused him to miss every Brazilian qualifier, so to come back in the tournament and perform so well was remarkable. In his prime, he was one of the deadliest strikers football has seen.

JOHAN CRUYFF

49 The Netherlands did not win the World Cup in 1974, yet pundits will tell you that the Dutch team was the more skilful and entertaining, and one of the main reasons for that was Johan Cruyff.

If you could pinpoint a highlight, it would perhaps be the famous Cruyff turn of 1974 when he looked to be kicking the ball forward, but instead scooped it backwards. It allowed him to turn tightly on the spot and head off in the opposite direction, leaving Sweden's Jan Olsen dumbfounded.

Such magic was also evident in the final. The penalty in the second minute, during which Cruyff barked orders and orchestrated a move that led to him being knocked to the ground and a goal scored. It was just a shame he retired from international football in 1977, fearing kidnap in Argentina.

BOBBY MOORE

50 Even if West Ham's centre-half had not captained England to glory in 1966, he would still have proved his worth with a stunning display in that tournament, as well as those which preceded and followed in 1962 and 1970. But it will be 1966 that he will always be remembered for.

He didn't score (he only ever got two goals for England and they were both in friendlies) but it was his floating cross that helped Geoff Hurst get the opener in the final, and his long pass which secured the infamous final Hurst goal that signalled it was all over.

What Moore lacked in pace and aerial ability, he made up for with his football brain, and he was widely seen to be the best defender of all time. Alf Ramsey didn't hesitate in making him captain even though he was aged just 22 years and 47 days. Moore repaid that faith in spades while becoming known as a gentleman of the game.

Skilled at free-kicks and frequently creating chances for Hurst, he was at his best on the big occasion, and people were so confident in his talent that Ron Greenwood, manager of West Ham, believed in 1965 that Moore would be reason for an England victory since he had planned so well for the win.

○ England captain Bobby Moore lifts the World Cup in 1966

© Getty Images

MOMENTS
30 JULY 1930

THE FIRST CHAMPIONS

Uruguay etch their name in history as the inaugural World Cup's winners

Every story has a beginning, and the story of the world's greatest sporting spectacle begins in 1930. That is the year in which the first World Cup was held in Uruguay, chosen as the hosts to coincide with the nation's celebration of the centenary of its first constitution.

The final was contested by Uruguay and Argentina in the Estadio Centenario, constructed especially for the tournament. Uruguay struck first, scoring in the 12th minute, but Argentina fought back and went into the break leading 2-1.

In the second half, Uruguay took control again, scoring three goals and running out 4-2 winners. They became the first team to lift the famous Jules Rimet trophy, and etched their name in football history. The next day was declared a national holiday to celebrate the success.

Uruguay's glorious moment is not only significant for its people, but for football fans across generations. The success of that first tournament ensured the World Cup continued, treating us to all the exciting moments, awe-inspiring players, shock defeats and wonderful goals we've witnessed over the years. Without the success of the first tournament, the World Cup wouldn't be what it is today.

○ Pelé lifts the Jules Rimet trophy after Brazil beat Italy in the 1970 final

PELÉ:
THE GREATEST

The rags-to-riches tale of the World Cup's most iconic star

Stardom can flash like a supernova, fading into the darkness of obscurity as quickly as it erupts. Only the greatest of stars to have graced football's grandest stage shine with the enduring brightness that assures their status as legends. In that elite group, there is one that burns brighter than any other: the North Star of the World Cup, Pelé.

Pelé's legend is a testament both to his own incredible talent and the power of the World Cup. He played most of his club football for Santos in his native Brazil. In an age where it wasn't possible for fans to watch live football from all over the world and find clips of the next young talent on YouTube, it may as well have been on Mars as far as most of the world was concerned. It was the World Cup that gave Pelé the platform on which to showcase his ability to a global audience – his blend of athleticism and technique, artistry and end product, intelligence, desire and supreme dribbling skill. That is why his story is so intimately intertwined with the history of the tournament. The World Cup trophy is the treasure he claimed to complete his archetypal rise from rags to riches: the tale of an impoverished young kid who became a national hero and sporting icon through his exploits. It is the tournament that made him – and with his supreme talent, he helped make the tournament.

Pelé made his World Cup debut in Sweden in 1958. At only 17 years old, he was the youngest player ever to play in the tournament. He was already a star in his native Brazil, having finished the 1957 season as the league's top scorer at only 16 years of age while playing for Santos, but now he had the chance to do something even more special.

Pelé, like the rest of his countrymen, had not forgotten the national trauma known as 'the Maracanazo', or 'Maracanã Blow'. The name refers to Brazil's shock defeat to Uruguay in the final game of the 1950 World Cup, held on its own soil in a Maracanã Stadium packed with 200,000 people. Pelé screamed at a picture of Jesus in his father's room after the fateful final, asking why Brazil was being punished and telling the image of Christ that if he had been there, Brazil would have won. In Sweden, he had the chance to make good on this pledge.

Pelé arrived at the tournament with a knee injury, and didn't play in Brazil's first two games, a 3-0 victory over

PRAISE FROM PEERS

Johan Cruyff, Barcelona and Holland star:

"PELÉ WAS THE ONLY FOOTBALLER WHO SURPASSED THE BOUNDARIES OF LOGIC"

Just Fontaine, French striker and top scorer in the 1958 World Cup:

"WHEN I SAW PELÉ PLAY, IT MADE ME FEEL I SHOULD HANG UP MY BOOTS"

Ferenc Puskás, Real Madrid and Hungary legend:

"THE GREATEST PLAYER IN HISTORY WAS DI STEFANO. I REFUSE TO CLASSIFY PELÉ AS A PLAYER. HE WAS ABOVE THAT"

Bobby Moore, 1966 World Cup-winning England captain:

"PELÉ WAS THE MOST COMPLETE PLAYER I'VE EVER SEEN, HE HAD EVERYTHING"

Michel Platini, France legend and Ballon d'Or winner:

"THERE'S PELÉ THE MAN, AND THEN PELÉ THE PLAYER. AND TO PLAY LIKE PELÉ IS TO PLAY LIKE GOD"

Austria and a 0-0 draw with England. He made his debut in his team's third group game against the USSR, impressing in a performance that included an assist for Vavá in a 2-0 win. Brazil moved on to the knockout stage, and it was here that the young Pelé began writing his legend in the lines drawn with his brilliant feet.

Midway through the second half in their quarter-final against Wales, and Pelé, standing on the penalty spot, received a headed ball on his chest with his back to goal. With a deft flick and turn, he left his marker floundering and poked the ball into the net. It was the only goal of the game, taking the team into a semi-final clash with France.

The France team of 1958 had some prolific talents of its own in the legendary Just Fontaine and Roger Piantoni. Indeed, both bagged a goal apiece – Fontaine in the first half and Piantoni in the second. This wasn't enough, however, to prevent the French from being swept away by an electric Brazil that netted five goals. Pelé led the charge, scoring in the 52nd, 64th and 75th minutes to become the youngest ever player to get a hat-trick in World Cup history.

In the final, Brazil came up against Sweden. That Brazil would win was far from a foregone conclusion: not only were Sweden the host nation, but no World Cup up to that point had been won by a nation outside its own continent. Sweden took the lead in the fourth minute through Nils Liedholm, but Brazil responded quickly, Vavá netting an equaliser – then

Opposition players at the 1966 World Cup in England decided that the best way to stop Pelé was to kick him

Pelé was injured in Brazil's second game of the 1962 World Cup and wouldn't feature again in the tournament

another – to take Brazil into the break leading 2-1. In the 55th minute, Pelé broke yet another record, becoming the youngest scorer in a World Cup final as he netted one of the tournament's greatest ever goals. Waiting in the box, Pelé held off his marker as he jumped to meet a cross, twisting in the air to direct the ball towards the penalty spot with his chest. Another defender came out to close him down, but Pelé lifted the ball over his head, watched the ball drop from the sky and volleyed it powerfully into the bottom corner. Mário Zagallo followed up on Pelé's wonder goal to earn Brazil a 4-1 lead, before Simonsson pulled one back to give the hosts a slither of hope. It wasn't to be, however, as Pelé sealed the victory in stoppage time with a looping header that left the onrushing keeper stranded. The whistle blew, and he broke down in tears of joy. The pain of the Maracanazo had been dulled, if not entirely healed. Brazil lifted its first World Cup trophy.

The 1958 World Cup triumph was a defining moment for both Pelé and Brazil. This victory helped establish Brazil as a global footballing superpower, and vindicated the nation's belief in a stylish brand of football that it wanted the world to admire. Indeed, the popular picture that now exists of what this great footballing nation represents – beautiful football, swashbuckling attacking, inspirational individual talent and international glory – started here. Pelé, at only 17, played an important part in that, making himself a star in the process. It was mind-boggling to see such a complete player at such

○ Pelé (top) celebrates with his teammates during Brazil's 4-1 win over Italy in the 1970 World Cup final

PELÉ FACTS & FIGURES

MOST SUCCESSFUL LEAGUE GOALSCORER WITH

1281 GOALS IN **1363 GAMES**

YOUNGEST WORLD CUP WINNER

ONLY PLAYER TO WIN **3** WORLD CUPS

19 NOVEMBER

IS PELÉ DAY AT SANTOS – AFTER THE DATE PELÉ SCORED HIS **1000TH GOAL**

SCORED HIS FIRST PROFESSIONAL GOAL ON HIS LEAGUE DEBUT AT **15** YEARS OLD

JOINT FIFA PLAYER OF THE CENTURY WITH **DIEGO MARADONA**

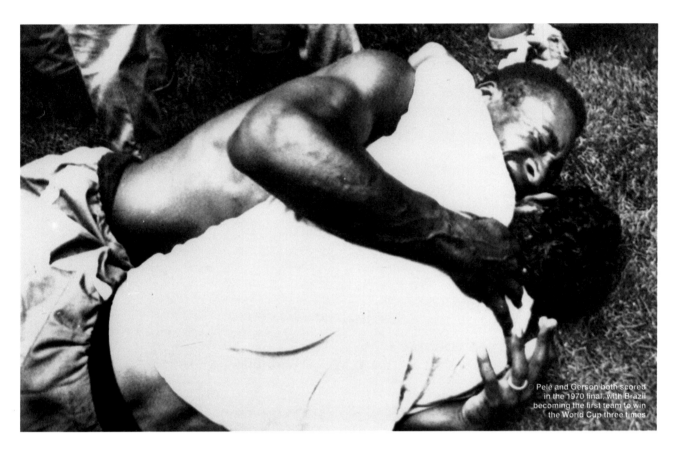

Pelé and Gerson both scored in the 1970 final, with Brazil becoming the first team to win the World Cup three times

a young age. He possessed pace, power, precise passing, vision, flair, a high work rate, anticipation, and an ability to finish. He had the whole world at his feet.

Yet Pelé's international career was not to continue in storybook fashion. When the 1962 World Cup in Chile rolled around, Brazil's star seemed primed to lead the team on to more glory. He started in apt fashion, creating one and scoring another after a mazy run where he beat four players in a 2-0 win over Mexico. In the next game against Czechoslovakia, however, Pelé was injured, keeping him out of the rest of the tournament. Fortunately, that Brazil side was hardly starved for talent, and Pelé's teammates took up the slack, in particular a fellow footballing genius by the name of Garrincha. Brazil went on to triumph without Pelé, defeating Czechoslovakia 3-1 in the final.

Pelé's reputation was not diminished despite his absence for much of the 1962 tournament, and he was still the world's most famous talent when he came to England to play in the 1966 World Cup. But again, Pelé suffered from injury problems in a tournament where opposition players had evidently decided to kick him out of the game. He scored one goal in the opening match, missed the second through injury, and returned in the final game of the group stages, where he ended up limping around the pitch as he watched his team fall 3-1 to Portugal.

The 1966 failure left a bitter taste in the mouths of Brazil fans and Pelé himself. He vowed he would never play for Brazil in a World Cup again, frustrated by the deliberate fouling he had been subject to and the injuries he'd suffered as a result. Eventually, however, Pelé was persuaded to return to play in the 1970 World Cup in Mexico. We're grateful he did, because the team that he became part of was to go down in history as perhaps the greatest World Cup side of all time.

The side that went to Mexico in 1970 was phenomenally talented. The standout player in defence was the great Carlos Alberto, fittingly for a Brazil team, because of his rampaging attacking talent. In central midfield, the cultured Gerson was there to pull the strings alongside the tireless Clodoaldo. On the left was the graceful Rivelino, credited with innovating the flip flap, and on the opposite flank another of Brazil's many all-time greats, the dynamic Jairzinho. He complemented Rivelino's tendency to sit deep with a direct, pacey approach and eye for goal. Partnering Pelé was Tostão, a player with skill, vision, and most importantly for his partnership with Pelé, the intelligence to interchange with his star teammate, dropping deep when necessary and pushing forwards to make space in the hole for Pelé when appropriate.

This gifted team went one down to Czechoslovakia in the 11th minute of their first game of the group stages. A Rivelino goal brought them in level at the break, and Brazil exploded in the second half to swat their opponents out of their way. Pelé struck first to give Brazil the lead and Jairzinho followed up with a double to finish the game.

Brazil's next match was against the world champions: England. Only one goal was scored in the game, but it was a classic nonetheless. Brazil's supreme attacking talent came up against a magnificent defence, Pelé leading his compatriots against a defiant Bobby Moore, who time after time would break up Brazil's attacks. Pelé could draw out the best of his opponents, it would seem. Indeed, he did just that when Gordon Banks stopped Pelé opening the scoring with a stop dubbed the 'save of the century'. Carlos Alberto played a cutting pass from deep, allowing Jairzinho to get behind the England defence. He made it to the byline and crossed to Pelé, who headed powerfully towards the bottom corner. It looked as if the header was already beyond Banks as he reached behind him and tipped the ball up over the bar.

But Pelé and Brazil were not to be denied. They kept coming, and in the 59th minute, broke England's resolve. Tostão danced into the edge of the England box and lifted the ball into the middle. Pelé killed it dead with a deft touch, then shifted it outside into the path of Jairzinho to power home into the top corner.

Brazil's final group game was against Romania. They rested a couple of stars, shifting Gerson and Rivelino to the bench, but Pelé remained, and would again have a key role to play. He opened the scoring after 19 minutes with an inswinging free kick, and added another in the 67th minute in a 3-2 victory that took Brazil into the quarter-finals.

Brazil ploughed through their opposition in the knockout stages. First to fall were Peru, Pelé assisting a goal for Tostão in a 4-2 win. Pelé created another in Brazil's next match, a semi-final against Uruguay that they won 3-1, and where one of Pelé's most famous moments took place. As Pelé raced to meet a through ball, Uruguay's goalkeeper rushed out to try and snuff out the attack. Just as Pelé and the ball met the keeper at the edge of the box, Pelé feinted as if he was going to collect the ball and try to round the keeper. Instead, he left the ball untouched, passing the bamboozled keeper on one side, the ball on the other. Pelé over-rotated after collecting the ball at a wide angle and sent his shot wide of the far post, but the moment is still remembered as a great illustration of Pelé's footballing brilliance, despite the miss.

The final of the 1970 World Cup took place at the Azteca Stadium in Mexico City. Brazil met their antithesis, an Italy side known for its 'Catenaccio', or 'door-bolt', defensive system. It was a game that, perhaps more than any other, would cement Pelé's legend. Fittingly, it was Pelé who opened the scoring in the 18th minute with a powerful header, the diminutive figure rising high in the air to beat his taller marker. Italy found a way back into the game through Boninsegna on 37 minutes, exploiting a loose pass at the back. It stayed 1-1 going into half-time. Gerson took Brazil back into the lead with a powerful long-range drive in the 66th minute, and was again involved for Brazil's third, sending a long ball floating into the opposition box. Pelé was there to meet the pass with the perfect cushioned header sent back across goal into the path of an onrushing Jairzinho to give Brazil a 3-1 lead. Brazil then signed off with a goal that epitomised the flowing attacking football that had made this 1970 team such a pleasure to watch. It was the perfect final flourish to cap off a phenomenal tournament, and a goal that was truly worthy of a World Cup final. Indeed, it would go down in history as one of the greatest team goals ever scored.

The move started after Brazil won the ball deep in their own half. After an exchange of passes, the ball ended up with Clodoaldo at the base of midfield. He danced his way past four Italian players to the delight of the crowd, and then laid the ball off to Rivelino on the left side of the pitch at the halfway line. Rivelino played the ball forward to Jairzinho, who had drifted over from the right flank. Pelé later said that this was a deliberate ploy – Italy were employing a man-marking system, so Jairzinho would periodically drift over to pull Italy left back Giacinto Facchetti out of position, opening a space on the right they called 'the avenue'. After receiving Rivelino's pass, Jairzinho cut inside and laid the ball off to Pelé in the middle off the pitch. He paused for a moment, holding the ball up while he waited for the right moment to release it. Then he nonchalantly slid the ball out onto the right, into 'the avenue' Jairzinho vacated and ran into the path of an onrushing Carlos Alberto. Alberto crowned the move by smashing the ball low into the far corner. The final ended 4-1. Attack beat defence. Beauty triumphed over austerity.

The 1970 trophy was Brazil's third, making them the most successful team in World Cup history. They cemented their status as a premier football nation, and did it with the characteristic style that made 'Brazilian' a byword for skill, technique and flair. Pelé was recognised as the star of that unbelievably talented team, and awarded the Golden Ball for player of the tournament. It was Pelé's last World Cup, and the perfect end for his special relationship with the competition.

The beautiful football with which the 1970 Brazil team wowed the world should give us cause to remember that the legend of Pelé should not overshadow the talents of his teammates. Players like the great Garrincha, who played alongside Pelé in 1958 and led his nation to World Cup glory in 1962 in Pelé's absence. Or the phenomenal Jairzinho, who scored in every game of the 1970 tournament. Yet, while recognising their greatness, it is telling that even among all that gifted talent, Pelé's teammates and rivals revered him as the best. He is the most complete player football has ever seen, and he is unquestionably the World Cup's greatest icon. He gave the tournament some of its greatest moments and, in return, it gave him his.

○ The 1970 World Cup-winning Brazil team would go down as one of the greatest in history

BREAKING NEW FRONTIERS

Pelé is credited as a pioneer in helping to grow football in the US. He originally retired from club football after the 1974 season, though he would continue to make the odd appearance for Santos.

In 1975, Pelé officially came out of retirement to join the New York Cosmos. This was not Pelé at his peak, but he was still enough of a star to bring a lot of public interest to the young North American Soccer League, the precursor to Major League Soccer. The club's increased profile led them to move from a sparse pitch that the club's groundsman spray-painted green to hide the lack of grass for Pelé's debut on TV in the Yankee Stadium.

By Pelé's final season in 1977, the Cosmos averaged crowds of around 40,000, which was by far the biggest in the league. In that year, Pelé, alongside new signing Carlos Alberto and Germany legend Franz Beckenbauer, led the Cosmos to the NASL championship.

TOP 10: SCORERS

They shoot, and they really do score. Here we take a look at the World Cup's all-time leading goalscorers

GABRIEL BATISTUTA

⚽ Aside from being a legendary player for Fiorentina, a club he represented from 1991 to 2000, Batistuta was – until Lionel Messi surpassed him – Argentina's all-time top scorer. He played in three World Cups, in 1994, 1998 and 2002, scoring 10 goals in 12 matches – a hugely impressive 0.83 goals per game.

GARY LINEKER

⚽ Lineker made his England debut aged 23 years and 176 days in 1984, the same season he scored 22 goals at Leicester City. He scored a hat-trick in his first World Cup tournament match against Poland on 11 June 1986, and he was joint third top scorer at Italia '90. Of his 48 goals for England throughout his career, 10 were at the World Cup.

HELMUT RAHN

⚽ The most important of Rahn's 10 goals in 10 World Cup tournament matches came against Hungary in 1954 – the one that sealed World Cup glory for West Germany. He also helped his country to the semi-finals in the 1958 World Cup, a tournament that saw him become joint second goalscorer with Pelé on six goals.

JÜRGEN KLINSMANN

⚽ Klinsmann was a constant fixture during the 1990s, with appearances at the 1990, 1994 and 1998 World Cups – first for West Germany, and then for the unified German team. He scored in each tournament, getting 11 goals in total. He also picked up a World Cup winners' medal in 1990, and went on to manage Germany to third place in 2006.

GERD MÜLLER

⚽ Gerd Müller was one of the most phenomenally efficient strikers in German footballing history. With 68 goals in 62 appearances for West Germany, Müller was Germany's all-time leading goalscorer for almost 40 years until he was surpassed by Miroslav Klose. However, it took Klose double the amount of caps to do so, highlighting Müller's incredible finishing ability.

PELÉ

⚽ **Pelé played in four World Cups: 1958, 1962, 1966 and 1970.** But what is perhaps most incredible is that he won all but one of them (1966), making him the only player to have lifted the World Cup three times. He scored 12 goals in 14 matches – remarkably, six of those goals in 1970 after he initially refused to take part.

JUST FONTAINE

⚽ **Fontaine played in just one tournament: 1958.** But what a time he had, sticking a staggering 13 goals in the back of the net despite playing just six games. That tally of 2.17 goals per game is pipped only by Sándor Kocsis (on 2.20) and yet, like Kocsis' Hungary, it still wasn't enough for France to win the tournament.

GREGORZ LATO

⚽ **One of the shining stars of Poland's golden generation of players.** He rose to fame in the 1970s and early 80s, Lato played for the Polish national side at five major tournaments, including a third-place finish at the 1982 World Cup in Spain. However, Lato's highpoint as an individual player came at the 1974 World Cup, where he was the leading scorer with 7 goals and the only Pole to-date to have won the honour.

RONALDO

⚽ **The Brazilian took part in four tournaments in 1994, 1998, 2002 and 2006.** He scored four in 1998, the year Brazil came runners-up to France, and he doubled that tally in 2002, scoring twice in the final. This not only got him a well-earned World Cup winners' medal, it cemented the Golden Boot award, and won him man of the match too.

MIROSLAV KLOSE

⚽ **Klose competed in 2002, 2006, 2010 and 2014.** But although his five goals in that first tournament helped get Germany to the final, they lost to Brazil. There was further misery when they came third twice in a row. How thrilled he must have been to finally lift the World Cup in 2014 – in which he scored just two of his record-breaking 16 goals.

LEGENDS OF THE '66 WORLD CUP

It's 1966 and all that: relive the iconic extra-time victory that brought football back home, as told by those who were there

Within hours, London's *Evening Standard* had hit the streets. 'Champions of the World', ran the headline. "A dream come true. England have won the World Cup," it began. The following day, the Sunday newspapers also picked up the news, inevitably splashing it across their front pages: 'Golden Boys!' the *Sunday Mirror* proclaimed, before adding a chirpy note to the world's bankers: "Britain's reserves went up yesterday by one valuable gold cup." There was no doubt this would be a day to savour for decades to come.

On 30 July 1966, 96,924 people packed into Wembley Stadium and 32.3 million British viewers tuned in on their televisions to watch England take on West Germany in the World Cup final. Today, the names of the England players who took part that day can be reeled off one by one like old friends. But back then – despite Alf Ramsey declaring, "we will win the World Cup" when appointed England manager in 1962 – not many fans really believed they could do it.

"I don't think England supporters expect England to win anything and there was certainly that same feeling even back then," says West Ham fan John James, who attended the final in 1966. And yet Ramsey stuck to his word. He had formally taken charge on 1 May 1963, and promptly began to do things his way. The lack of control over team selections suffered by the previous manager, Walter Winterbottom, was not for him. Ramsey made his own choices, and whether that was naming Bobby Moore as England captain at just 22 years old, or playing without wingers in the face of disbelief, he stood by every decision he made.

As hosts, England automatically qualified for the 1966 FIFA World Cup, along with defending champions Brazil. That left 14 other places which were taken by Argentina, Bulgaria, Chile, France, Hungary, Italy, North Korea, Mexico, Portugal, Spain, Switzerland, Uruguay, the Soviet Union and West Germany. All of England's games were held at Wembley and, while the team started slowly with a 0-0 draw against Uruguay, they then went on a sensational run of victories that took them straight to the final.

Bobby Moore lifts the Jules Rimet trophy aloft in one of the most enduring images in English sporting history

world cup legends

The night before the big day, Ramsey – with a nagging sense that the occasion could overwhelm his men – tried to help the players relax. Without fanfare, they went to watch *Those Magnificent Men in Their Flying Machines* at a local cinema. "Alf loved going to the pictures so we all strolled down to the picture house," recalls winger Terry Paine, who had just achieved promotion to the First Division with Southampton and played against Mexico in the second game. "And you know what? Not one photo was taken or autograph was asked. Can you imagine that today? You wouldn't get within 100 metres of anybody but that was a remarkable feature of football in those days."

It wasn't the first time Ramsey had tried to relieve anxieties among the squad. You could say it had become a speciality of his. After that group stage draw, he took the players to Pinewood Studios. "We mixed with stars such as Sean Connery and went on the set of the James Bond film," says Paine. "That was extra special and it got us over the disappointment." Ramsey treated the international side as if it were a club team. He adopted similar principles to those that had seen him turn Ipswich Town into league champions at the first time of asking. The team became close-knit and fostered a feeling of togetherness that would serve them well on the pitch.

On the eve of the final against West Germany, most of the talk concerned striker Jimmy Greaves and whether or

LEGEND OF MANAGEMENT: SIR ALF RAMSEY

What Alf Ramsey lacked in pace and height, he more than made up for with an uncanny knack for ensuring he was in the right part of the pitch at the right time. He made his professional debut on 26 October 1946 in a second division game for Southampton against Plymouth Argyle and proved himself to be an intelligent right-back. But after 96 appearances for the club, scoring eight goals, he left for Tottenham Hotspur and won the first division in 1951.

When his playing days were over, Ramsey went on to manage Ipswich Town in the Third Division (South) in 1955, leading them to promotion as champions. He won the first division with the club in 1961-62, an incredible success that led to him managing England. After winning the World Cup in 1966, he took England to third place in the UEFA European Championship in 1968 but quarter-final defeats at the 1970 World Cup and 1972 Euros, coupled with failure to qualify for the 1974 World Cup were disappointments that saw him sacked by the FA.

○ Ramsey was inducted as a manager into the English Football Hall of Fame in 2002 and again as a player in 2010

not he would play in place of Geoff Hurst. For most of the tournament Greaves had partnered Roger Hunt up front, but an injury granted Hurst a place in the team for the quarter-final. Hurst scored the only goal in that game and went on to provide an assist for Bobby Charlton in the semi. Unwilling to change a winning side, Ramsey decided to overlook Greaves for what would have been the biggest game of his life.

"Being a West Ham fan, I was pleased that Hurst was going to be involved in the final," says James. "The atmosphere for the games had also begun to change for the better. It had been quiet in the earlier rounds. For the final, there was a fabulous atmosphere. There were lots of Germans in the stadium – we were surprised at how many – but they were well outnumbered. It was something to behold."

Back then, the fans didn't wear replica kits. They just weren't available to buy. Neither did they fly the flag of St

○ The leather ball used in the 1966 World Cup final, originally claimed by West Germany's Helmut Haller

○ George Cohen and Jack Charlton in action during the 1966 World Cup final

George, preferring the Union Flag instead. The supporters also turned up with their England rosettes proudly pinned to their clothes, swinging their rattles and making a tremendous noise. "It was very different to the guys with their drums and trumpets today," says Arsenal fan Roy O'Neil, who recalls buying his ticket from an agency at the Barbican in London for five times its face value, and ending up in a neutral zone of the stadium surrounded by Italian fans. "I remember the game being the first time I had heard the clapping routine which is still used today; the one that ends in the shout "England". It was unique at the time."

The game got underway at 3pm. England versus West Germany; Bobby Charlton pitted against Franz Beckenbauer; Bobby Moore marking the first victory in winning the coin toss and electing to kick off. The crowd were in high spirits and then, in the 12th minute, Helmut Haller cut the atmosphere completely dead. A cross from Sigfried Held was knocked from the head of Ray Wilson to his feet, allowing the German to fire a low cross-shot to Gordon Banks' right: 1-0 to West Germany. Just six minutes later, however, Moore sent a free kick flying over the German defence, into space created by Hurst. With a glancing header, he equalised.

England were playing tremendously well. "As a Liverpool fan, I was impressed with Hunt up front, or Sir Roger Hunt as he has always been known at Anfield," enthuses Dr Rogan Taylor, director of the Football Industry Group at the University of Liverpool. Hunt fired directly at the German

goalkeeper Hans Tilkowski but just couldn't quite get it past. "The team were all playing their part and no one was letting the side down," says O'Neil.

But the crowd started to quieten as the minutes ticked away. "The fans didn't do much to lift the team at this point, I remember that quite starkly," says Manchester United fan John Toye. "But they began cheering again once Martin Peters scored to put England ahead again." It was the 78th minute and Peters shot from close range, having initially hit Horst-Dieter Höttges from a Hurst attempt.

AFRICA PULLS OUT

Unfortunately, there were no sporting legends from Africa in the World Cup of 1966. Every team in the continent decided to pull out of the qualifiers in protest at the teams which topped the African zone having to play-off against European or Asian opposition for their place in the finals.

The feeling was that Africa should be offered a direct route for qualification, and the boycott led to the rules being changed for the 1970 tournament. One consequence of this action was that North Korea took part in the World Cup for the first time in 1966, which caused problems at home: the country wasn't recognised by the UK, and so it was almost refused entry. Today, six of the 32 finalists are taken from Africa.

world cup legends

With five minutes to go, the players who hadn't been selected to play in the team that day had assembled on the touchline on the orders of Ramsey and they were fully anticipating a win. They were all part of the team, Ramsey had told them, and so they must be supportive of those on the pitch. They waited for the referee to blow his whistle and then – drama.

In the 89th minute, moments after a narrowly wide shot by Charlton had England fans groaning, Wolfgang Weber shot towards the England goal. It crossed the line and the crowd went completely silent. "What a gut-wrencher at the stroke of full time," says James. It was 2-2 and that meant only one thing: an agonising extra 30 minutes. "No way did we think the team would win in extra time. The team was dejected but Alf came out, waved his finger and gave them a lecture." It seemed to do the trick.

The rest of the squad remained in situ for the duration of that half and, unlike James, Paine was confident. "I still believe Gordon Banks was the greatest goalkeeper the world has seen, he was a superstar," he says. "Bobby Moore was one of the best defenders there has ever been – he didn't have pace but his soccer brain was second to none. Ray Wilson could match Brazil's Garrincha for pace and Nobby Stiles was of the old school and did a great job. Martin Peters was an intelligent guy coming in from the left-hand side. Bobby Charlton speaks for himself. And young

Alan Ball, the best one-touch player in the world. Then we had Geoff Hurst alongside the hard-working Roger Hunt."

Ball crossed to Hurst in the 101st minute and Hurst smashed the ball on the underside of the crossbar, causing it to bounce down on to the line and be cleared. But did it go in? Referee Gottfried Dienst consulted his linesman Tofiq Bahramov. "I remember him running over to this day," says Paine. "The Russian linesman said something which sounded like it would be 'yes'. The goal was given and from our point of view it was in."

The West Germans tried to rally but England were on a high. Some supporters ran on to the pitch and at home, viewers listened to a distracted Lancastrian BBC commentator named Kenneth Wolstenholme utter the infamous words: "Some people are on the pitch! They think it's all over!" Hurst blasted into the net and the crowd went wild. "It is now!" England had won the World Cup.

All across the country, people jumped in celebration. "I was only ten and watched it in our front room on our old battered black-and-white set while my mum went shopping," says Manchester United fan John Horne. "After the game, I went outside and repeatedly smashed the ball against our coal shed wall for the next three hours, imitating Geoff Hurst's winning goal." The result meant so much to so many people and enthusiasm for football soared among the population.

As Haller sneaked away with the match ball, whipping

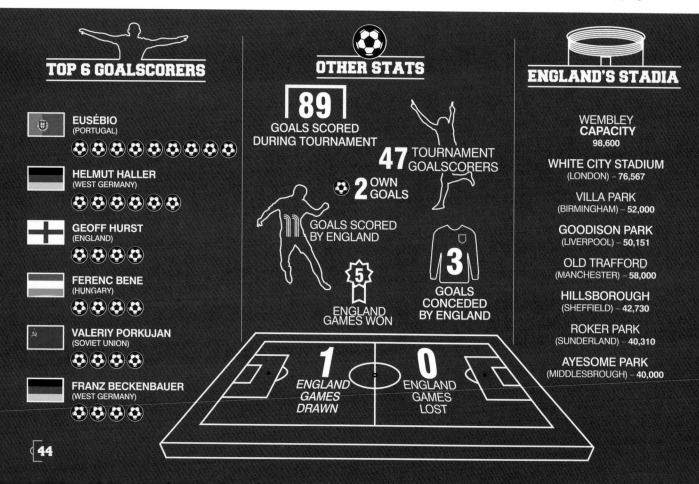

TOP 6 GOALSCORERS

EUSÉBIO (PORTUGAL)

HELMUT HALLER (WEST GERMANY)

GEOFF HURST (ENGLAND)

FERENC BENE (HUNGARY)

VALERIY PORKUJAN (SOVIET UNION)

FRANZ BECKENBAUER (WEST GERMANY)

OTHER STATS

89 GOALS SCORED DURING TOURNAMENT

47 TOURNAMENT GOALSCORERS

2 OWN GOALS

GOALS SCORED BY ENGLAND

5 ENGLAND GAMES WON

3 GOALS CONCEDED BY ENGLAND

1 ENGLAND GAMES DRAWN

0 ENGLAND GAMES LOST

ENGLAND'S STADIA

WEMBLEY **CAPACITY** 98,600

WHITE CITY STADIUM (LONDON) – 76,567

VILLA PARK (BIRMINGHAM) – 52,000

GOODISON PARK (LIVERPOOL) – 50,151

OLD TRAFFORD (MANCHESTER) – 58,000

HILLSBOROUGH (SHEFFIELD) – 42,730

ROKER PARK (SUNDERLAND) – 40,310

AYESOME PARK (MIDDLESBROUGH) – 40,000

A beaming Queen Elizabeth presents Moore with the World Cup trophy following the game

it from under Hurst's nose as he celebrated his hat-trick, the celebrations continued in the dressing room. "I got to the door of the England dressing room just as Bobby arrived carrying the gleaming, real Jules Rimet trophy", says sports historian and former *Daily Express* chief football reporter Norman Giller, who recalled the entire day in a comprehensive book called *July 30 1966: Football's Longest Day*. "All the England players were in a state of exhaustion as they pushed their way down the tunnel, yet Bobby looked immaculate without a bead of sweat."

Giller went to hug the captain in congratulation of the feat but Alf Ramsey appeared, irked by the disputed goal, and the journalist knew it was time to leave. Ramsey's spirit quickly lifted but the players were still in disbelief. "Will somebody pinch me," George Cohen was heard as saying.

"Am I dreaming?" He wasn't. The players went to a reception at The Royal Garden in Kensington but the fans weren't ready to give up celebrating. As they got wind the players were at the luxury five-star hotel, they gathered outside, cheering as their new heroes appeared on the balcony.

The excitement lasted for weeks. Frank Wood, a reporter on the *Bolton Evening News*, recalled fans wanted to pay tribute to England's newest footballing legends. "There was one guy who twice walked the Pennine Way who suggested that all the stiles along the 250-mile route should be known as 'Nobbies'". That didn't happen but it didn't matter. The players had secured their place in history; the most successful England side of all time. "To win a World Cup, you need at least five world-class players," says Paine. "We probably had more than that." Result.

LOSING THE WORLD CUP

Although England achieved success in 1966, they actually managed to lose the World Cup – in the most literal sense. The trophy was stolen on the afternoon of 20 March 1966 from the Methodist Central Hall in Westminster where it had been put on display. It led to a nationwide hunt and much embarrassment for the FA but it also heralded another sporting legend: Pickles, a black-and-white collie, who sniffed out the Jules Rimet Trophy seven days later wrapped in a newspaper in a hedge in London.

"It was all over the news because there was this mystery element to it", recalls screenwriter Michael Chaplin, who based the TV drama, *Pickles: The Dog Who Won the World Cup*, on the story in 2006. "It was almost like a classic Ealing comedy – this ridiculous event whereby this iconic piece of silverware was taken and no one knew who did it. I thought it was charming; a British caper which lent itself well to an entertaining film."

ROAD TO THE FINAL

After a stuttering start, England were rampant en route to the World Cup final

ENGLAND 0 – 0 URUGUAY

11 JULY, ATTENDANCE: 87,148

If there was any optimism that England would win the World Cup, it faded during this lacklustre opening game in which they came up against a disciplined Uruguay side that was so defensive-minded England failed to score for the first time at Wembley since 1945. For their efforts, Uruguay were booed from the field by frustrated England fans but their players celebrated as if they had been victorious because they sensed a draw against one of the favourites would help them through to the next round. As it happened, England had only a handful of goalscoring chances, with Jimmy Greaves having the majority of them, but their build-up play was uninspired and lacking pace and they left the field looking exhausted.

○ England were continually frustrated during their opening game

ENGLAND 2 – 0 MEXICO

16 JULY, ATTENDANCE: 92,570

The game against Mexico reignited the confidence of both the England team and the crowd. It also marked the tournament debuts of Terry Paine, who replaced Manchester United's John Connelly, and Martin Peters, who came in for the injured Alan Ball. England left the pitch winners thanks to goals in either half by Bobby Charlton, with a thunderous 25-yard shot, and Roger Hunt, who finished tidily from close range. The win – along with Mexico's previous draw with France – all but ended their opposition's hope of progression and got England on their way.

ENGLAND 2 – 0 FRANCE

20 JULY, ATTENDANCE: 98,270

This game belonged largely to Roger Hunt, primarily because he scored both England's goals in their 2-0 win. In doing so, he ensured England would progress, but perhaps just as remarkable was Gordon Banks' third clean-sheet of the tournament. Nobby Stiles got himself into some bother following a vicious tackle which led to calls by FIFA officials for him to be dropped. Ramsey refused but he couldn't ignore a larger problem: one of the biggest star players, Jimmy Greaves, was injured and had to be sidelined. It would turn out to be his last game of the tournament.

○ Nobby Stiles' tough tackling against France didn't go over well with FIFA

"A VICIOUS TACKLE BY STILES LED TO CALLS BY FIFA OFFICIALS FOR HIM TO BE DROPPED"

ENGLAND 1 – 0 ARGENTINA

23 JULY, ATTENDANCE: 90,584

In Argentina this game has since been referred to as 'el robo del siglo', or 'the theft of the century' because the goal – by Geoff Hurst, who was brought in for the injured Jimmy Greaves – was deemed by them to be offside. It also saw the Argentinian captain, Antonio Rattin, sent off for a second caution, incidents that began to cause bad blood between the two sides. It wasn't a particularly violent match, but Rattin refused to leave the field, holding the game up by ten minutes. As he left, he grabbed the corner flag – bearing the Union Jack – and screwed it up. Argentina held on admirably but Hurst's 78th-minute header was timely and decisive, taking England through.

ENGLAND 2 – 1 PORTUGAL

26 JULY, ATTENDANCE: 94,493

Eusébio was renowned as one of the world's best players and he ended the tournament as the top scorer with nine goals. It was against him and his Portugal team that England faced their fiercest test, not only letting in their first goal of the tournament but being as mesmerised by the finesse of the Portuguese attack as the watching crowd. Even so, it was England who scored first; Bobby Charlton getting the goals in the 30th and 80th minute with Eusébio only responding in the 82nd minute, making for a tense finale to the match. It was a true test for England's defence, though, and also a good lesson in sportsmanship. There was an admirable air of grace in the behaviour of the Portugal players throughout.

Moore and Stiles embrace after England's hard-fought semi-final victory over Portugal

THE GERMAN ROUTE

The West Germans played their games at Hillsborough in Sheffield and Villa Park in Birmingham, starting in the best way possible with a 5-0 thumping of Switzerland before a crowd of 36,127. They were then held to a scoreless draw against Argentina but recovered their attacking prowess by putting two past Spain in a 2-1 victory that saw them advance straight to the quarter-finals.

Their opponents were Uruguay and while the South Americans had played a frustrating game against England with an eight-man defence, they proved more susceptible to the German onslaught. West Germany fired four goals past them without reply in a thrilling game at Roker Park in Sunderland. Much of that was to do with

two Uruguayans being sent off, however. For that 'crime', it was the home nation who got it in the neck: the referee was from the UK and this only heightened anti-British feelings among the South Americans. It didn't help matters that a German defender, Karl-Heinz Schnellinger, had clawed the ball from the top corner of his goal using his hand to prevent Uruguay from scoring early on and had suffered no penalty for having done so.

West Germany went on to face the Soviet Union in the semi-final at Everton's Goodison Park and won 2-1. Helmut Haller and Franz Beckenbauer got the goals for the German side while Valeriy Porkujan pulled one back in the final two minutes to make for a more respectable scoreline.

THE GOAL THAT NEVER WAS?

For more than 50 years, England's third goal in the final has proved controversial, with doubt cast over whether the ball crossed the line after it hit the crossbar and bounced down. While the goal stood following consultation between the referee and the linesman, the Germans have always believed it should have been ruled out.

In 2010, it appeared scorer Sir Geoff Hurst himself thought the same. He told a press conference to promote sponsorship of the Football Conference, "I have to admit that the ball didn't cross the line". But it later emerged it was an April Fool's joke, much to everyone's relief.

Thankfully, in 2016 Sky Sports used the EA Sports Performance system to prove once and for all that it did cross the line. Or maybe not. BILD Sports of Germany continued to dispute the claim and there have been tests which show the opposite is true. A decision set to go into extra time itself, perhaps.

b The ball is cleared but Roger Hunt wheels away in celebration. After a lengthy pause, the referee signals a goal

1 Nobby Stiles collects the ball centrally and sprays a pass out to the right wing

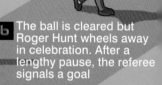

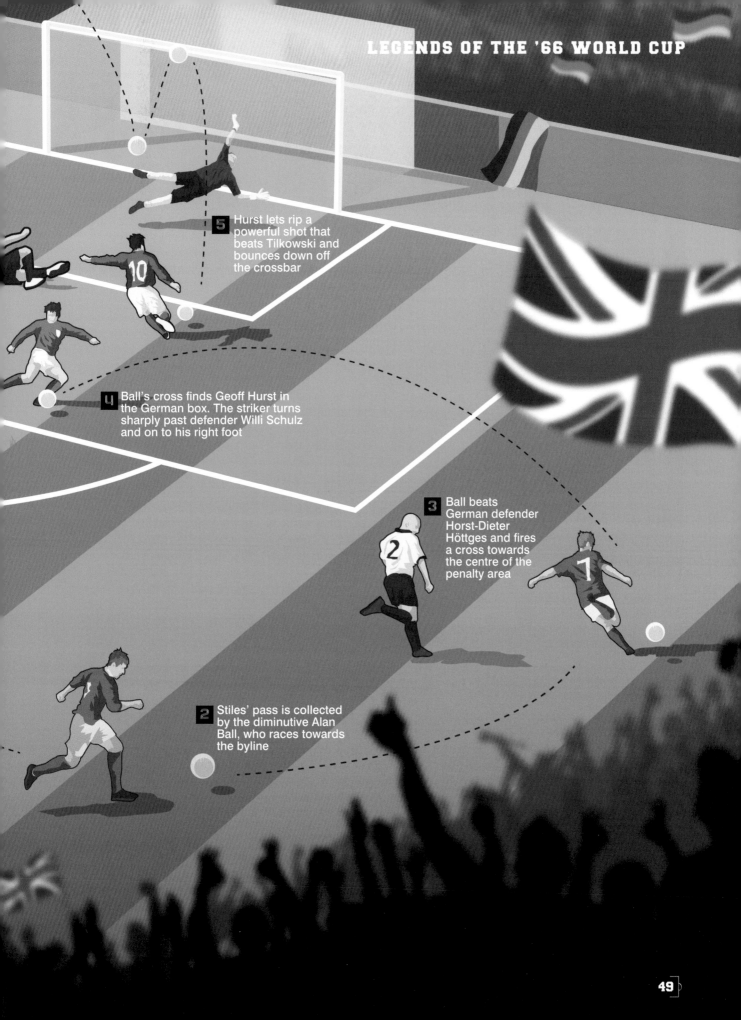

5 Hurst lets rip a powerful shot that beats Tilkowski and bounces down off the crossbar

4 Ball's cross finds Geoff Hurst in the German box. The striker turns sharply past defender Willi Schulz and on to his right foot

3 Ball beats German defender Horst-Dieter Höttges and fires a cross towards the centre of the penalty area

2 Stiles' pass is collected by the diminutive Alan Ball, who races towards the byline

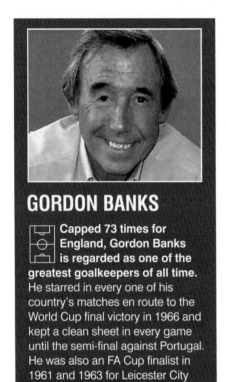

GORDON BANKS

Capped 73 times for England, Gordon Banks is regarded as one of the greatest goalkeepers of all time. He starred in every one of his country's matches en route to the World Cup final victory in 1966 and kept a clean sheet in every game until the semi-final against Portugal. He was also an FA Cup finalist in 1961 and 1963 for Leicester City and a winner of the League Cup in 1964 with the Foxes and Stoke City in 1972. He sadly passed away in February 2019, but he will forever be remembered for his heroics on the pitch and his kind, warm demeanour off it.

GORDON BANKS

Arguably England's greatest ever goalkeeper, Gordon Banks recalls that fateful day in 1966 in this exclusive interview

The 1966 World Cup started well from your perspective, but did you sense it could be an uphill battle from then on?

When we drew 0-0, I thought, "Wow, we have our hands full here now. We have really got to do something". But I think there was tension in that first match and we didn't play like I knew we could play. It was only when we won the next match and then got through the group stage that we realised we stood a bit of a chance. We were undefeated and we weren't conceding goals and we felt teams would be saying, "Oh crikey, they are hard to score against." That was good.

Having four cup finals under your belt, you were no stranger to Wembley, were you?

We also played England friendlies at Wembley and it did give me a little bit of confidence to go out and do my job. There's not much difference between playing in a [domestic] cup final and a World Cup final – you just need to go out there, do the best you can and hope everything goes your way.

Is it true that Alf Ramsey managed the England national team as if they were a club side?

He made it that way, definitely. He also made sure that if he told you something you had to do it or you were out. Oh yes, he was pretty strong in that sense. But the information that he got over to the players was fantastic. He would give you the strength and the weakness of the opposition. He might come over to me and say 'go and watch this centre forward, he's got a great left foot and if it's on that side he can really wallop it so be prepared because he will definitely do it'. He was a terrific manager, and something really special.

Were you nervous?

Well, we tried to do what we would normally do for a friendly match but when four or five us decided to walk from Hendon Hall hotel into the village, people recognised us and they were coming over and wishing us the best of luck, which showed how important this game was. There was also a large crowd outside the hotel where the bus was waiting and when we got on the bus, everyone was clapping and cheering – that brought a lot of tension. I mean, I know it was the same route that we always took when we played international games at Wembley but all of that meant it was very quiet on the bus.

Was there a point when you thought, this is it: there is a real chance that you could be making history?

When the noise went in the dressing room to tell us that it was time to go into the tunnel, then wow, that was when it really hit home. We saw the Germans alongside us and shook their hands but walking down that tunnel was really nerve-wracking. The tension was very high. But after we sang the national anthem, tossed the coin and I ran to the goal to have one or two practice shots lined up against me, the referee blew his whistle and that's when the tension disappeared. We just concentrated on doing our jobs. We wanted to give it 90 minutes as best we could.

Germany put one past you very early in the game. What was your feeling at that point?

Well, to be honest with you – and I'm not being critical because he's a great player and he did well for the team – but I'm pretty sure if Big Jack [Charlton] had not been standing in front of me, I would have saved the shot. But I couldn't see. He was just inside the six yard box. I don't know what he was doing and I'm not the kind of guy to give people rollickings or things like that but anyway, yes. It never put our heads down, though. We just realised we had to carry on and get a goal back

Was there a real strength of mind among the players – a will to win?

We were all concentrating on what we were doing. I was also watching and hoping we would get an equalising goal, which we did – and then we went in front.

Which players stood out during the game?

You've always got players who stand out for their clubs and for England, like Bobby Charlton and Bobby Moore.

○ Banks and his England teammates attempt to keep out a West German attack

They stood out tremendously. Alan Ball was voted by players as the best that day because of the amount of effort he put in and the way he kept possession and so on. He had a super day. But I think the rest of the lads were just class players and we played as a team, if you understand. We didn't play as individuals. Bobby Charlton, who could hit a ball fabulously with both feet, if he couldn't get a shot in, he wouldn't try for a shot and waste it, he would keep possession and make a pass. So there were these terrific players and you couldn't really say anything wrong about them to be honest.

How did you feel when Germany got that second goal to equalise right at the death?

Well, nobody mentions this and I can't believe it but if you watch that goal again, you will see me and Bobby Moore chasing the referee for a few yards. They'd got a free kick which was about 25 or 30 yards outside of the box on my right-hand side and they came down to the edge of the box to about 25 yards and took a short free kick. They then started to run in towards my goal and the ball came right across, into their paths. One of the players, Karl-Heinz Schnellinger, was running and the ball was just behind him. I don't think he did it deliberately but it hit his arm, which is a foul – had it not hit his arm, it would have gone right across and off for a throw on the other side for us. But it rolled right into the path of the guy [Wolfgang Weber] who got the equaliser. I tried to block it but he took it well over my body and he knocked it in. It should have been a free kick for us.

That forced the game into extra time; is that where Alf Ramsey came into his own?

Alf – a great manager – was something special, I tell you. He really was. Both teams had been running and working hard in that 90 minutes and both managers were on the pitch. I was farthest away but as I got close, I could see the German players sitting on the

pitch and three or four of our lads doing the same. I then heard Alf say, "Get up, chin up, we don't want to make it look as if we're tired". He was trying to get something over on them and he wanted to get their players to think, "They must be very fit, they don't want to sit down". That was typical of Alf. Something like that might just help.

Did the players react well to that?

We looked at each other and thought that was a good idea. And then he said "Come on, you've won this once, you have to get out there and win it again". That was all he said really. He knew we were playing quite well and well enough to get that result.

Extra time was dramatic, wasn't it?

Oh yes. And while there was a big furore about Geoff's goal that hit the bar, the thing that always stands out in my mind is that Roger Hunt, who was standing nearest when the ball came down and saw it, didn't go to head it. The goalkeeper made the dive and he was on the floor and you would have thought Roger would have made sure but he didn't because he saw it go over the line and thought they would give a goal. I like the thing I saw on Sky Sports this year [in 2016] which showed the ball was just over the line. That shows Roger Hunt was right. It was a goal.

Geoff Hurst secured the game with a hat-trick. What do you remember of that goal?

I was like all the defenders, shouting at Bobby Moore to whack the ball up the field. "Get rid of it!" Bobby saw Geoff running on his own and he popped

the ball right into his path. Of course the Germans had been attacking in numbers so they had very few people back there. So Geoff made this run and scored but I will never forget him saying, "I just wanted to thump it. It wouldn't have worried me if it had gone way over the bar because it would have taken a lot of time to get the ball back." He knew there was not long to play but the ball went into the top corner. And that was it. It was all over.

Could you relax then?

Yes. I could see the people walking from the stand and going home. They knew it was the end and I knew that would be it then. But I just couldn't believe it. West Germany were a terrific side and they had some great players who could play some very good football. Running around with that trophy on our ground with our supporters was fantastic. Bobby Moore let each one of us have a little run with it and we would wave it to the crowd. But when we came round to the German supporters – and this is true – they were all clapping us and I thought, wow, that is really something nice and different.

Was that unusual?

Oh yes, crikey. Very rarely did fans clap the opposing team, so that was really nice. But our fans were fantastic too. I remember we were close to finishing our meal at the hotel after the game and Alf came over and said, "come on you lads, we have to go out on this balcony. There's a crowd out there." The fans were clapping and roaring and the police had to close the road. It was incredible; a great day.

MOMENTS

23 JULY 1966

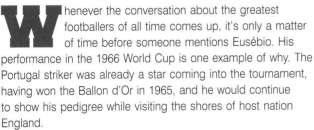

EUSÉBIO NETS FOUR

One of the all-time greats stakes his claim as a World Cup legend

Whenever the conversation about the greatest footballers of all time comes up, it's only a matter of time before someone mentions Eusébio. His performance in the 1966 World Cup is one example of why. The Portugal striker was already a star coming into the tournament, having won the Ballon d'Or in 1965, and he would continue to show his pedigree while visiting the shores of host nation England.

The Black Panther was on characteristically lethal form, netting three goals for Portugal in the group stages to help them to wins over Hungary, Bulgaria and Brazil. In his team's quarter-final against North Korea, however, he really stepped up to the plate. Portugal looked like they were going to get knocked out of the tournament by underdogs North Korea after going 3-0 down within 25 minutes. Instead, Eusébio dragged them out of trouble, netting four consecutive goals in a phenomenal performance and leading his team to a 5-3 victory.

For two of his goals, Eusébio used his pace to latch onto balls played into the box, and finished emphatically, one of which was a particularly tasty effort placed perfectly in the top corner. Either side of his third goal were two converted penalties, both put away confidently and comfortably. Eusébio would add to his four-goal haul in Portugal's next game when he scored against England. However, they lost that game 2-1, and were eliminated. Eusébio finished as the tournament's top scorer with nine goals.

MARACANAZO:
A 'NATIONAL CATASTROPHE' FOR BRAZIL

Before winning five World Cups Brazil suffered a trauma it can neither forget nor truly confront

Everywhere has its irremediable national catastrophe, something like a Hiroshima. Our catastrophe, our Hiroshima, was the defeat by Uruguay in 1950."

This insight into the Brazilian national psyche offered by the late Nelson Rodrigues, one of the country's most distinguished playwrights, is a useful one for non-Brazilians.

How does one explain what was seen immediately after the Seleção's humiliating 7-1 defeat to Germany in the semi-final of the 2014 World Cup? If it had happened to England at Wembley, or to the French at the Stade de France, you might expect stunned silence and perhaps even some booing. But on 8 July 2014, the Mineirão stadium in Belo Horizonte was the picture of collective grief. Television cameras captured images of fans weeping in the stands, eyes skyward, while the men in yellow jerseys sank to their knees.

The first thing to understand is that Brazilians had been through it already, before the world had ever heard of Neymar, Ronaldo or even Pelé.

Brazil were heavy favourites for the tournament of 1950, the first World Cup in 12 years due to war in Europe. Not

The Brazil team of 1950 lines up before their World Cup clash with Mexico, which they won 4-0

only did Brazil boast some of the world's best attackers, but they were also the hosts.

The home team played all but one of its matches at the new Maracanã stadium, which had been specially built for the tournament. Construction had been hit with severe delays, meaning matches kicked off as work was still being done to the new hulking monolith.

According to contemporary reports, concrete rained from its roof during a 21-gun salute in the opening ceremony. Nonetheless, the Maracanã was looked upon with immense pride in Brazil, a country which strove to challenge Europe's sporting hegemony. It was a politically important moment for Brazil too.

The government of the day, led by President Eurico Gaspar Dutra, believed that a home World Cup win would unite the population behind his often tumultuous regime and portray the rapidly industrialising country as a new world power.

Although they had never won a World Cup before, Brazilians were confident of their footballing pedigree and were unafraid of hype. The new footballing philosophy, distinct from those of European nations and neighbouring Argentina and Uruguay, was also beginning to take form.

Later termed 'jogo bonito', the style emphasised free-scoring attacking play and eschewed the more underhanded – and perhaps nasty – elements of traditional South American football. They had won the previous year's South American Championship, the precursor to the Copa América, at a canter, scoring almost six goals a game.

The Seleção duly raced through qualification for the 1950 World Cup's second phase. Scoring eight goals and conceding just two in three matches, Brazil topped their opening group, which also featured Yugoslavia, Switzerland and Mexico.

Although the format of the World Cup has been changed countless times over the decades, the 1950 tournament remains the only one for which the winners were not decided by a final knockout match. Rather, the destination of the Jules Rimet trophy would come down to a round robin between group winners Brazil, Sweden, Spain and Uruguay.

Buoyed by their encouraging early tournament performances, the home side raised their level by several gears for the final group stage. Sweden and Spain were dispatched 7-1 and 6-1 respectively, with forwards Ademir and Chico running riot.

The final group match was to be played against Uruguay, who had already beaten Sweden but were held to a 2-2 draw by Spain. Brazil knew a draw at the Maracanã would see them crowned world champions. According to estimates, just under 200,000 fans – or about a tenth of the population of Rio de Janeiro – piled into the ground to witness Brazil's presumed coronation.

Moacir Barbosa, the Brazilian goalkeeper, carried the blame for the defeat for the rest of his life

○ Uruguay's victorious side of 1950 won their country's second World Cup following the triumph on home soil in 1930

THE MAN WHO DIED TWICE

In the aftermath of the Maracanazo defeat it was Brazil's three black players – Moacir Barbosa and defenders Bigode and Juvenal – who took the majority of the flak.

Despite being considered one of the world's greatest goalkeepers, Barbosa was made to suffer more than anyone else.

Roundly blamed by fans and journalists for an error that allowed Alcides Ghiggia to score Uruguay's winner, he would play only once again for his country.

When the Maracanã installed new goalposts in the 1960s the old wooden ones were given to Barbosa. His decision to burn them did little to exorcise his demons; his reputation as Brazil's bogey man haunted him for the rest of his life.

Barbosa once recalled that in 1970, the year in which the country won its third World Cup, he noticed a mother point

him out in the street, telling her child that he was "the man who made all of Brazil cry".

Barbosa was even reportedly barred from visiting a national team training camp near Rio de Janeiro in 1993 ahead of a World Cup year. Administrators apparently feared he would bring the players bad luck.

Speaking to a journalist shortly before his death in 2000, Barbosa said, "In Brazil, the most you get for any crime is 30 years. For 50 years I've been paying for a crime I did not commit. Even a criminal when he has paid his debt is forgiven. But I have never been forgiven. I am not guilty. There were 11 of us."

An emotional Brazil fan reacts to the 7-1 defeat by Germany during the 2014 World Cup

Such was the local confidence that a samba band stood pitch-side throughout the Uruguay match, ready to play a new song – *Brazil the Winners* – on the full-time whistle.

A number of local newspapers, assuming nothing would go wrong, even began calling the side the 'Champions of the World', while Rimet, the then-FIFA President for whom the World Cup trophy was named, prepared a congratulatory speech in Portuguese.

Incredibly, 22 gold medals, each one inscribed with the names of each Brazilian squad member, had reportedly already been made, while the mayor of Rio de Janeiro delivered a rousing pre-match speech in which he "already saluted the team as victors".

Alcides Ghiggia, Uruguay's star winger, later said, "It was a fantastic atmosphere. Their supporters were jumping with joy as if they'd already won the World Cup.

"Everyone was saying they'd thrash us three or four nil. I tried not to look at the crowd and just to get on with the match."

Brazil began more brightly than their southern neighbours,

imposing themselves on the match and creating a number of chances. Although the first half ended 0-0, the home side found themselves a goal up just two minutes into the second period.

However, their lead only lasted until the 66th minute, Ghiggia getting the best of his marker to find a yard of space before whipping in a fierce delivery that was steered home by Juan Alberto Schiaffino. Uruguay had equalised, and they soon found themselves on the front foot.

With just over ten minutes remaining, the diminutive Ghiggia picked up the ball once more and hurtled down the wing and into the Brazilian penalty area. He shaped to cross, as he had done countless times that afternoon. Preparing to meet the delivery, Moacir Barbosa, the Brazilian goalkeeper, moved a fraction towards the centre of his goal, leaving a crack of space open between himself and his near post. Ghiggia spotted the chance and rifled a low right-footed shot into the net via the post. He would later comment that, "Three people have silenced the Maracanã – Frank Sinatra, the Pope and me."

With Brazil unable to find an equaliser Uruguay were crowned World Cup champions for the second time. Despair swept the ground like wildfire. Tales later emerged of a number of distraught fans spontaneously taking their own lives by leaping from the stands.

Arthur Nemesio, a Brazilian fan who attended the match, described the scene to *The Guardian* in 2014,: "There were a lot of people crying. A lot of men, women, boys, girls crying. It was the saddest day in the history of Brazilian football."

It's hard to overstate the collective impact of the 1950 World Cup on Brazil. Five subsequent World Cup wins have failed to expunge the memory of the match, forever known as Maracanazo, and it is commonplace for Brazilians to refuse to discuss it openly.

Carlos Alberto, a Brazilian World Cup winner in 1970, once said that the failure to win on home soil will always haunt his country.

"We had the chance to win," he said. "It's always important to win at home, like England won in 1966, like Germany won in 1974, like Argentina won in 1978. For us Brazilians, it was a mark that stayed, which no one can erase."

Yet out of the misery a new steeliness was born in Brazilian football, as were the Seleção's iconic canary-yellow jerseys. The white strips the team had worn in defeat to Uruguay would never be seen again after 1953.

Pelé later said one of his earliest memories were of his father's tears after the Maracanazo. "My father told me that you have to win the World Cup for Brazil," he said. In Sweden eight years later, aged just 17, he would do just that.

TOP 10: KEEPERS

It's not often that goalkeepers are the hero – so often they find themselves the villain – so here's 10 of the very best to have graced the world stage

MANUEL NEUER

⚽ There aren't many players across professional sport that manage to revolutionise any one aspect of the game. However, Manuel Neuer is certainly one of those select few. His "sweeper-keeper" style of play and the speed he displays when rushing out of the box to anticipate opponents has changed defensive goalkeeping across the board, as well as earned him the accolade of goalkeeper of the decade from 2011 to 2020. He won the 2014 World Cup with Germany, earning a Golden Glove in the process.

JOSÉ CHILAVERT

⚽ Goalkeepers have a reputation for being frustrated outfield players, and Chilavert could not be caged. None of his eight international goals came at a World Cup, but he was the first keeper to take a direct free-kick at the competition, almost scoring against Bulgaria.

CLÁUDIO TAFFAREL

⚽ With more than 100 caps for Brazil, Cláudio Taffarel helped his national side find success at the 1994 World Cup as well as a couple of wins at the Copa América along the way. His main attributes were his explosive power as well as his penalty saving ability, with three in a single game against West Germany.

FABIEN BARTHEZ

⚽ Laurent Blanc used to kiss his goalkeeper's bald head for good luck before every game – and in 1998 it seemed to work. His five clean sheets helped France to a famous home victory, and his 10 shutouts in 17 appearances are a World Cup record, shared with Peter Shilton.

DINO ZOFF

⚽ At 40, Zoff was the oldest man to win the World Cup when he captained Italy to glory in 1982. Despite his age, his reflexes left nothing to be desired: his late save from Oscar in a quarter-final against Brazil was one of the greats.

LEV YASHIN

⚽ **Not many men can claim to have revolutionised the position of goalkeeper, but 'The Black Spider' was among the first to marshal his defence rather than merely block the ball.** He also played in four World Cups for the Soviet Union and won the Ballon d'Or in 1963.

GIANLUIGI BUFFON

⚽ **'Gigi' seems to embody everything that is great about the World Cup.** A fiercely proud Italian, he is the most capped player in his country's history, and in 2006 topped the world while conceding no goals from open play and being chosen as goalkeeper of the tournament, then the Yashin Award.

IKER CASILLAS

⚽ **The Casillas home has quite the trophy cabinet, but among five Spanish league titles, three Champions Leagues and two European Championships, one medal has pride of place: the 2010 World Cup winners' medal.** Not only that, but he was the man to lift the trophy as captain.

GORDON BANKS

⚽ **Apart from winning the 1966 World Cup, Banks is also responsible for one of the greatest saves in the tournament's history.** In a game that would decide Group 3, Brazil legend Pelé nodded the ball downwards towards the bottom corner of the goal, only to be stunned when Banks leapt across to divert it behind for a corner.

OLIVER KAHN

⚽ **No goalkeeper had ever won the Golden Ball before Kahn's triumph in 2002.** Twice Kahn brilliantly denied Robbie Keane in a group stage clash and in the last-16 fixture against Paraguay, Kahn produced at least one and perhaps two world-class saves in a 1-0 win. And in the final, the imperious Ronaldo might have had four had it not been for Kahn.

MOMENTS

7 JUNE 1970

TWO ICONS SWAP SHIRTS

Brazil's Pelé and England's Bobby Moore swap shirts in a famous show of respect

The 1970 World Cup was host to one of the competition's finest games, a match between the World Cup holders at the time, England, and arguably the greatest World Cup side ever fielded, the 1970 Brazil team. The game's close also provided us with one of the World Cup's most iconic images, when Brazil legend Pelé swapped shirts with England captain Bobby Moore.

The match itself was closely fought, Gordon Banks' most famous save denying Pelé a goal when he flicked his header up over the bar, and England squandering several good chances. One of the key features of the game was the battle between the incredible attacking talent of Brazil – the likes of Jairzinho, Rivelino, Gerson and Pelé – and England's

defence, led by Bobby Moore. The former came out on top, with Brazil getting a 1-0 victory.

After the final whistle, Pelé and Moore embraced, swapping shirts in a sign of mutual respect. The two clearly admired each other's talents – indeed, Pelé would later call Moore the best defender he ever faced – and the gesture was intended to acknowledge how good they each knew the other was after a competitive match. The warm smiles they both wore as they conversed led to the moment being praised as an example to follow as to the spirit in which the game should be played: two rivals who had given everything they had engaging with sportsmanship, dignity and friendship.

DIEGO MARADONA:
ARGENTINA'S GOLDEN BOY

Genius, saviour, cheat: Maradona has been called
many things by many men, but he remains 'El Diego'

It would be quite possible, although not entirely
plausible, to devote the entirety of this ode to El Diego
to that one goal. No, not *that* goal, the other one. The
second one. The decade-defining 11 seconds of brilliance
that left the England team strewn across the field of the
Azteca in the hot sun, wondering what they had to do to
stop the little Argentinian. The truth was that they weren't
the first, they wouldn't be the last, and few would ever find
a solution.

Having taken his first professional bow as a 14 year old,
it certainly did not take the national team long to recognise
Diego Maradona's talents. He made his senior debut
in 1977 at the age of 16, the youngest Argentinian
international ever.

However, probably wisely given his later predilections
for distraction, manager César Luis Menotti (known as 'El
Flaco' – 'the slim one') did not pick him for the 1978 home
World Cup because he felt he was too young. It didn't seem
to hinder his side, who lifted the trophy after beating the
Netherlands in the final.

When Maradona did make it to football's biggest show,
he was a world away from the teenager whom El Flaco had
left out.

But Barcelona pounced just before the rest of the world
could see what Maradona was about. In 1982, he was sold
for a world-record fee of nearly double what Boca had paid
for him just 12 months previously. Perhaps if Barça had
waited, they might have put their cheque book away again.

With Argentina playing their first game of Spain '82 at the
Camp Nou against Belgium, the stage was quite perfectly
set for the Argentinian to make good the disappointment
of missing out in 1978 and simultaneously win over his
new fans in Catalonia. He came within inches of a fairytale
moment, a second-half free kick hitting the crossbar, but
otherwise Argentina were stodgy and disappointing, going
down 1-0. Maradona was greeted with a level of on-field
aggression bordering on out-and-out violence.

The squad was uncomfortably tense, inside and out.
Plenty of the experienced 1978 champions had been
retained beyond usefulness and it had not gone unnoticed:
Minotti was slammed in the Argentinian press for remaining

Maradona triumphantly
holds the trophy after the
1986 World Cup final between
Argentina and West Germany

Maradona would see red against Brazil in 1982, with Argentina crashing out in the second round

El Salvador and in the second group stage, they returned to Catalonia.

But there was no redemption for Maradona, whom Italy defender Claudio Gentile repeatedly hacked down in a 2-1 win. The referee appeared unconcerned and even booked Maradona, who was fouled a record 23 times in the game, for dissent. "Football is not for ballerinas," said the typically hard-nosed Gentile after the game.

Having already lost two of four games, the champions' clash with the imperious Brazil side was something of a foregone conclusion. Even the manner of it could be written ahead of time. And Maradona, full of four years of frustration at his own national side and three weeks of being kicked up and down the pitches of Spain, was unable to contain his frustration any longer. With Argentina trailing 3-0, Maradona aimed a kick at the ball and Brazilian midfielder Batista, who had just caught Argentina's Juan Barbas in the head with his studs. Maradona was promptly sent off. It was an unfair and ignominious end to his first World Cup. His new city booed him off the pitch. The disappointment only served to inspire Maradona to make his mark on the next tournament four years later.

Given that he had utterly failed to win over any Barça fans with his World Cup performances and perhaps even turned some against him, it is unsurprising that his two-year spell with the famous club was something of a struggle. Despite his 38 goals in 58 appearances, Maradona fell out with a number of senior figures at the club, contracted hepatitis, suffered a horrific ankle break that "sounded just like a piece of wood splitting" and developed a serious and persistent cocaine habit.

loyal to older players and deploying the younger Maradona in a deeper role. They even questioned whether the Falklands conflict, which officially only ended the day after the defeat to Belgium, was affecting the players. (Maradona recalled that the Argentinian media had been largely censored with regards to the war and that when the team reached Spain, they read that they were very much losing a conflict they had been told they were winning.)

But better news was to follow for the Buenos Aires press – on the pitch at least. Maradona was virtuosic in the second match against Hungary, scoring his first two World Cup goals. That 4-1 win was followed by a 2-0 victory over

THE HAND OF GOD

Maradona had started the move with typical flair in midfield before Jorge Valdano miscontrolled his pass, only for Steve Hodge to help the ball on its way towards goal. Maradona did the rest, punching the ball past England goalkeeper Peter Shilton with what Tunisian referee Ali Bin Nasser believed to be his head. It became an iconic moment.

Nasser's decision to allow Maradona's punched effort in the 1986 World Cup quarter-final haunted him for the rest of his career. He never refereed at a finals again and his efforts to blame linesman Bogdan Dochev turned into a slanging match, with each accusing the other. Maradona meanwhile, he later revealed, was hissing at his teammates to celebrate, because manager Carlos Bilardo had warned

them not to celebrate any goals to save energy in the hot Mexican sun – but Maradona was worried that the unusual behaviour might alert the referee to the foul play.

In the post-match press conference, Maradona cheekily said the goal had been scored by the head of Maradona and "the hand of God", coining the phrase by which the controversial strike would become known. It intensified what was an already fierce footballing rivalry and Argentina seemed to relish the pain the controversy inflicted.

○ After missing out on Argentina's 1978 World Cup victory, Maradona finally got his hands on the ultimate prize in 1986

○ Following wins over Greece and Nigeria in the 1994 World Cup, Maradona was banned from the tournament after testing positive for ephedrine

In the summer of 1984, Maradona broke the world transfer record again and headed to Napoli where, if he was not already developing a God complex, he would find ample ammunition. He was greeted by 75,000 adoring fans at the famous Stadio San Paolo. They immediately stripped club legend Giuseppe Bruscolotti of the captain's armband and gave it to Maradona. And when Argentina came to the 1986 World Cup in Mexico, the 25 year old was well and truly peaking.

Qualification had gone well. Maradona had scored three times and he had been made captain by manager Carlos Bilardo, a man whom he would come to call a mentor before a 2010 falling out.

The group draw pitted them against Italy, who had contributed to their downfall four years previously. After being publicly nullified by the violence of the 1982 World Cup, Maradona's growth in reputation had only served to ensure that teams would redouble their efforts to injure him. Just as Pelé had been in 1966, Maradona was a marked man. He would go on to draw more fouls at that World Cup than any other player in history.

In the opening game of the tournament against South Korea, Maradona found himself tripped, kicked, pushed and even punched around the pitch. One player even managed to get his studs through Maradona's socks and bandaged legs to draw blood. Undeterred, and more used to the treatment after two years in the Italian league with Napoli, Maradona did not kick back. The South Koreans were beaten 3-1, with Maradona providing assists for all three goals.

Next came Italy, who did enough to take an early lead from the spot, only for Maradona to get on the scoresheet for the first time in the tournament, beating the keeper with a perfectly placed volley. The points were split and Argentina's 2-0 win over Bulgaria – Maradona only had a hand in one of the goals this time – was enough to send them through at the top of Group A. And once they had beaten South American neighbours Uruguay 1-0, in which FIFA had warned Uruguay about potential trouble in the game and duly quashed much of the physicality against Maradona for 90 minutes at least, they were pitted against England.

That game has had more written about it than perhaps

any other. Four years after the Falklands War, this was the rematch that Argentina wanted with a rival they already had plenty of reasons to hate. But it is a testament to the quality of what followed that it can be remembered overwhelmingly for footballing reasons.

Generous commentators would call England's defence 'resolute' or 'single-minded', others would favour 'heavy-handed'. Terry Fenwick was immediately booked for an ugly foul on Maradona that seemed to set a standard for the game, and the Argentine star created a number of good chances that forced Peter Shilton into action. The warning signs were there and six minutes after the break, he skipped past four England players before Steve Hodge inadvertently chipped the ball towards his own goalkeeper, only for Maradona to punch the ball past him and into the net. The referee thought it was a header. His was the only opinion that mattered.

While his first goal may have been controversial, his second was unforgettable. Four minutes after the first, in the space of 11 seconds, Maradona slalomed past Peter Reid, Terry Fenwick and Terry Butcher before beating Shilton with a feint and scoring one of the greatest goals in World Cup history.

For Argentina, that game was bigger than winning the World Cup. It was about avenging 'Las Malvinas' and sinking the English World Cup warship. For many fans, the rest of 1986 is a blur of Maradona skills. He gained more personal redemption for 1982 in the semi-finals, scoring two exquisite goals to reach the final. Once there, it looked as though Argentina would be able to seal victory without Maradona adding too much. West Germany's Lothar Matthäus was his shadow and while the odd pass and flick helped Argentina to a 2-0 lead, Maradona wasn't as integral as in previous rounds.

But in seven second-half minutes, the West Germans fought back to level the game and pushed on for a winner, desperate to avoid extra time in gruelling conditions. However, that allowed Maradona all the space he needed. Six minutes from time, with the Germans overextended in attack, he split the defence with a delicate pass and set Jorge Burruchaga free. Minutes later, Maradona was lifting the Jules Rimet Trophy and the Golden Ball, both richly deserved.

The only thing harder than winning the World Cup is retaining it. But in 1990, it looked as though Argentina might be about to do just that. By now, Maradona had led Napoli to two Serie A titles, a Coppa Italia and a UEFA Cup – but his off-field behaviour, particularly drug use, had never improved, although he had not yet failed a substance test.

Italy were the hosts, a country who had kicked Maradona out of the tournament eight years ago. But, for an already injury-ravaged Argentina squad, things started disastrously. They scraped through the group stages after a shock loss to Cameroon and were pitted against Brazil in the second round. With Maradona carrying an injury, another kicking ensued at the hands of their South American rivals. However

MARADONA: THE MANAGER

It does not always ring true that the best players make the best managers. In fact, it often seems to be the opposite. Certainly, Maradona's lifestyle did not appear to be a natural fit with the job.

His most prominent spell as a manger came from 2008 to 2010, when he took over the national side in Argentina – despite having not worked as a manager since that ill-fated mid-'90s spell. Unsurprisingly, it would prove a turbulent time.

His fourth game in charge saw Argentina equal their record defeat, a 6-1 loss to Bolivia that left them staring down the barrel of failing to qualify for the 2010 World Cup. But he rallied a side bursting with attacking talent – Sergio Agüero, Lionel Messi and Juan Román Riquelme were joint top-scorers for the side – to seal qualification… and promptly told the media to "suck it and keep sucking it" on live TV. A two-month ban and hefty fine followed.

The World Cup itself went swimmingly, with four straight wins before they were thrashed 4-0 by Germany in the quarter-finals. Maradona wanted to stay on, but was eventually sacked and accused national team director Carlos Bilardo of betraying him as a parting shot.

he was still able, in the dying minutes, to produce a moment of quality, running through the Brazilian midfield before putting Claudio Caniggia through on goal.

Maradona's roller coaster World Cup continued in a shootout in the quarter-final: after failing to score against a Yugoslavian team who had ten men for 100 minutes, his tame shot was saved only for his teammates to spare his blushes and put them through. The semi-final against Italy went to penalties too, but in front of his home Napoli crowd, Maradona stepped up to take the fourth spot kick, a carbon copy of his last except that it beat Walter Zenga and Argentina went through to the final where the mighty West Germany waited.

The Germans had lost two finals in a row, and with Maradona limping and Argentina stuttering, they would rarely get a better chance to make amends.

There was an acceptance in the media that at 29 years old, living as he did and with the injuries he had been through, Maradona was unlikely to play another World Cup. Already, his body was not the one that had led Argentina to victory in 1986. But those looking for a glorious exit to underline his place in the World Cup hall of fame were left sadly wanting that night in Rome.

It was known as one of the dirtiest finals in World Cup history, and would only be eclipsed in 2010 by the Battle of Johannesburg. Maradona had admitted beforehand that they,

MARADONA FACTS & FIGURES

312 GOALS SCORED IN **590** PROFESSIONAL GAMES ACROSS THREE COUNTRIES

16 MOST APPEARANCES AS CAPTAIN AT A WORLD CUP

23 FOULED MORE TIMES THAN ANY ONE PLAYER IN A WORLD CUP MATCH (23 TIMES VS ITALY AT SPAIN '82) AND IN ONE WORLD CUP (53 TIMES AT MEXICO '86)

21 STARTED 21 CONSECUTIVE MATCHES FOR ARGENTINA AT FOUR WORLD CUPS

34 GOALS SCORED IN **91** INTERNATIONALS FOR ARGENTINA

GOLDEN BALL FIRST PLAYER EVER TO WIN THE GOLDEN BALL AT UNDER-20 AND SENIOR WORLD CUP – LIONEL MESSI IS THE ONLY ONE SINCE

24 BROKE THE WORLD TRANSFER RECORD TWICE BEFORE THE AGE OF 24

© Maradona scores one of the greatest goals in World Cup history against England in 1986

with four players suspended and he himself walking wounded, would need a miracle to turn over the Germans, and in truth it never looked likely. And it was rendered nigh-on impossible when substitute Pedro Monzón was sent off just after the hour mark. Andreas Brehme's 85th-minute penalty and Gustavo Dezotti's second yellow card only served to fulfil the inevitability of the result and absolve West Germany for the sins of two previous final defeats.

Maradona sobbed his way through the presentation ceremonies, a broken man whose mighty talent had begun to wane, crying for himself as much as anyone else.

But that was not to be the end of his World Cup story, although his 1994 appearance would be best forgotten. He had left Napoli under the cloud of a 15-month drugs ban – his cocaine habit had finally been caught out – and a one-year spell back with Carlos Bilardo at Sevilla did not work out. His weight was ballooning, his behaviour more out of control and he had barely played for Argentina. But a new-look Argentina team, without Maradona, had ended up in a World Cup play-off against Australia just to qualify for USA '94 and the country begged for him to be picked. El Diego was happy to answer

their prayers. He played little part in a 2-1 aggregate win, an Alex Tobin own goal proving the winner in Buenos Aires.

But the pressure proved too much. In February, he pulled out of the squad. However, he soon changed his mind and was handed the captaincy for the tournament. In the opening game, Maradona scored a goal filled with emotion. After a quick passing move with Greece already well beaten at 2-0 down, Maradona hammered the ball into the top corner. The image of him running towards the camera, eyes rolling back in his head and body convulsing maniacally, is one of the abiding memories of the World Cup.

After a win in the next game against Nigeria, Maradona left the field with a nurse escorting him to the drug-testing facility. That was how one of the World Cup's most talented and most flawed stars left the field for the last time.

He tested positive, although not for cocaine – for ephedrine, which he claimed had been in a power drink, the label of which he had not read. FIFA did not buy the excuse and sent him home. Argentina crashed out in the second round against Romania. Maradona was deemed a disgrace. He would play just 31 more games of football.

Maradona raises his hands to the heavens from a box at the Saint Petersburg Stadium prior to Argentina's Group D clash with Nigeria during the 2018 World Cup

Napoli fans mourn the passing of a man they hailed as a god

For a footballing genius forever haunted by demons and weighed down by a burden of expectation no mortal could shoulder forever, it was a fittingly tragic end to a playing career that transcended what had previously been thought possible.

With his boots finally hung up, and a brief but unsuccessful first spell in management behind him, Maradona remained in the grip of the one constant in his life: cocaine. In 2000 he collapsed in Uruguay as a result of hypertension and an irregular heartbeat caused by his addiction. Narrowly avoiding death, Maradona would move to Cuba in 2002 in a bid to finally kick the habit that was destroying him. Yet despite eventually freeing himself of drugs, health problems were never far away. Neither was the spotlight.

In 2005 Maradona hosted the first episode of a talk show titled *The Night of the No. 10*, interviewing his long-time friend and rival Pelé. High-profile figures including Fidel Castro and Mike Tyson would follow, each playing second fiddle to Argentina's favourite son, who inevitably proved to be a ratings sensation. But despite his success in the world of media, the pull of Maradona's one true love proved irresistible, and in 2008 he returned to management as head coach of the Argentina national team (see boxout on page 67).

Following a mixed World Cup campaign in South Africa in 2010 that had initially promised much but ended in a 4-0 hammering at the hands of a rampant Germany, Maradona found himself cast out after the Argentinian Football Association reneged on the offer of a contract extension.

Spells managing five different clubs in the UAE, Argentina

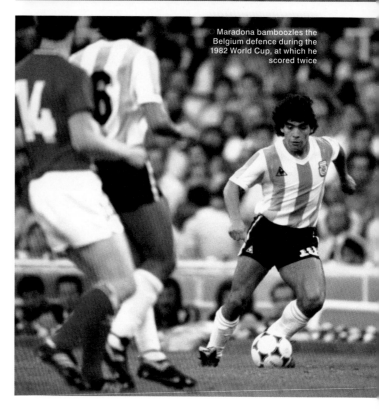

Maradona bamboozles the Belgium defence during the 1982 World Cup, at which he scored twice

and Mexico followed, but the incredible success Maradona enjoyed as a player never transferred to the dugout. In 2019 he took charge of Gimnasia de La Plata, a team located in Buenos Aires Province. It would prove to be his last.

On 25 November 2020, Diego Armando Maradona, the rebellious magician who had lit up the world with a ball at his feet, died at the age of just 60 in his home in the Argentine capital, a heart attack robbing him of life and the world of an icon.

Tributes poured in from every corner of the footballing community and beyond for a man many consider to have been the greatest player to ever grace a pitch. Among those to pay their respects was Pelé. "I have lost a dear friend, and the world has lost a legend. One day, I hope we will play football together in the sky."

It is often the fate of those who change the world to be taken before their time, and Maradona, the rambunctious pioneer who escaped the slum to conquer the world, had seemed exhausted by life for some time. And yet he always had a ready smile for everyone he met, be they an awed fan or a fellow professional. For he was, above all else, a man of the people. His people. After all, the most beautiful thing about Maradona, aside from his god-like ability, was that he wore his flaws with pride. No one has ever so perfectly illustrated what it is to be without equal and yet simultaneously just like everyone else. It is this trait, above all else, that makes the boy from Buenos Aires immortal.

REMEMBERING DIEGO

 Whether you loved him or loathed him, one thing you could never do was ignore Diego Armando Maradona.

There are many things you can say about El Diego, but his ability with a football at his feet will always be the most important. He was the greatest player of his era and arguably the best player of any era.

He lit up the 1980s with his breathtaking skill and ability and reached unbelievable highs on an international level with Argentina and at club level first with Barcelona and then at Napoli.

He single-handedly drove Argentina to World Cup glory in Mexico in 1986, and if there were ever to be a 90 minutes that defined Maradona's career it would be the quarter-final at the Azteca Stadium against the old enemy of England.

In between the 51st and 55th minute Maradona showed the two sides of his game and personality, firstly when he made up for the height advantage England goalkeeper Peter Shilton had over him by punching the ball into the net before running off to celebrate as if he had scored with his head – a goal he later called 'the Hand of God'.

Then minutes later he received the ball in his own half from Hector Enrique and proceeded to go on a 60-yard run past Peter Beardsley, Peter Reid, Terry Butcher (twice) and Terry Fenwick before slotting the ball past Shilton in what is regarded as the greatest individual goal ever scored. Two goals remembered for very different reasons.

Maradona again scored twice in the semi-final win over Belgium before going on to lift the World Cup after Argentina beat West Germany 3-2 in the final.

If what he did with Argentina made him a football great, then his achievements with Napoli made him immortal.

He guided the unfancied Neapolitan side to two Scudettos and a UEFA Cup during the late 80s and early 90s – a feat that has never been matched.

Yes, his career, and life, were blighted by cocaine, cheating and craziness, and yes, Pelé may have scored more goals and Lionel Messi won more trophies, but when you saw Diego Maradona with the ball at his feet then nothing else mattered. He was a genius.

James Andrew
Editor, FourFourTwo

MANAGING GREAT EXPECTATIONS:
10 LEGENDARY WORLD CUP COACHES

There have been 20 World Cup-winning managers, but which of those stand out the most?

Coaching an international football team is rather different to managing a club side. For starters, those at the helm are unable to plug any gaps in their squad by splashing the cash. There is also far less time to iron out problems on the training pitch or in regular fixtures.

Indeed, with international management, there is a greater reliance on organisation and trust. It's important to manage egos and plan for the long term while bearing in mind that any disappointments can linger for months between matches. At the same time, coaches have the weight of expectation of their entire country on their shoulders. No wonder such jobs are widely seen as the toughest in football.

Yet, if carried out with success, they can lead to great prestige. Winning the English First Division title with Ipswich Town, just a year after gaining promotion from the second tier, was a tremendous achievement, for instance. Yet manager Alf Ramsey is more fondly remembered for winning the World Cup with England in 1966.

At the same time, the very best managers in the club game can have the shine taken off them at international level, no matter how fleetingly. Alex Ferguson managed Scotland to the 1986 World Cup following the death of Jock Stein, but his team ended up bottom of Group E with defeats against Denmark and West Germany, and a draw against Uruguay. Nobody said it was easy.

It's with this in mind that we look at the ten most legendary coaches in World Cup history, and it wasn't easy boiling them down. Sepp Herberger, for instance, masterminded West Germany's World Cup win in 1954, with his side defeating the runaway favourites Hungary 3-2. Juan López Fontana won the cup for Uruguay on Brazilian soil.

But what we have here are ten coaches who have made a huge impression on the tournament for the numerous reasons that we go on to explain. Ever since Alberto Suppici won the inaugural competition in 1930 with Uruguay, the eyes of the world have been upon men such as these, with only one of our top ten coaches now looked upon more with disdain than the respect that he undoubtedly deserves.

That, however, is football, and the measure of expectation. Just as every England manager feels duty-bound to bring the World Cup back to the country that invented football, so past triumphs and the club achievements of the world's greatest players add an extra layer of burden for the managers. It's a funny old game, after all.

VITTORIO POZZO
THE ONLY COACH TO WIN TWICE

Although Vittorio Pozzo managed Italy for 19 years over three spells between 1912 and 1948, the man known as 'Il Vecchio Maestro' – 'the Old Master' – ensured his legendary status in the mid-to-late 1930s.

Having created the Metodo tactical formation – a 2-3-2-3, dubbed the W-W because of the shape it formed on the pitch – he led the Azzuri to World Cup victory twice, in 1934 and 1938. In doing so he became the first and only manager to lift the trophy twice.

As if to show just how great he was as a manager, he supplemented that by steering his team to Olympic gold in Berlin in 1936 – a victory that supporters of Italian dictator Benito Mussolini claimed was vindication of the fascist system's superiority.

But Pozzo had actually fallen in love with football in socialist-leaning Manchester, where he had studied at the turn of the 20th century. He was inspired by Manchester United's centre-half Charlie Roberts, who he regarded as the best player in the world.

Indeed, it is understood that Roberts influenced the style that Pozzo went on to adopt. He placed a greater reliance on the inside forwards rather than the centre-half, and this unleashed Internazionale's Giuseppe Meazza and Juventus's Giovanni Ferrari, both of whom – along with Eraldo Monzeglio – are the only Italians to have won two World Cups. Although Italy did not compete in the first World Cup in 1930, his team lifted the Central European International Cup that year.

He also controversially brought South American-born Italian nationals into the team, pointing to their role in the Italian army as justification. At the 1934 World Cup in Italy, they beat the USA 7-1 in the first round, overcame Spain 1-0 in a quarter-final replay and saw off Austria in the semi-final, beating Czechoslovakia 2-1 after extra time in the final.

Thanks to his dedication and determination, however, Pozzo sought to improve the team for 1938 in France, building it around Meazza and Ferrari. They beat Norway 2-1 in their opening match, before knocking out the hosts in the quarter-final 3-1. They then defeated Brazil in the semis and put four past Hungary in the final, conceding two to become victors once again.

FRANZ BECKENBAUER
THE MAN THEY CALL 'DER KAISER

As a player, Franz Beckenbauer captained West Germany to World Cup glory in 1974. He also led Bayern Munich to three European Cups and earned himself the nickname 'Der Kaiser' – 'The Emperor'. His stock kept rising after he stopped playing.

Appointed the team supervisor of West Germany in 1984 because he lacked a coaching qualification, he nevertheless took his unfancied team to the World Cup final in 1986. And while they ended up on the losing side against a Diego Maradona-inspired Argentina (beaten 3-2 in front of 114,600 people in the Estadio Azteca, Mexico City), the experience proved invaluable for the next tournament.

After coming a comfortable second in the qualifiers, they found themselves at Italia '90, topping Group D before beating the Netherlands, Czechoslovakia and England to reach the final. Once again their opponents were Argentina, but this time they had Jurgen Klinsmann, Lothar Matthäus and Rudi Völler.

Beckenbauer, who had also shown his natural leadership qualities in 1974 and stopped that team from falling apart, used his immense tactical insight and tight, organised footballing discipline to thwart their opponents, winning 1-0. In doing so, he became only the second man after Mário Zagallo of Brazil to win the World Cup both as a player and manager.

O In 1990, assistant Berti Vogts said Beckenbauer had only been a "proper coach" for two years, but it didn't prevent him winning the World Cup

Vicente del Bosque took Spain to the 2010 and 2014 World Cups

VICENTE DEL BOSQUE
A GENTLE WINNER

By the time Vicente del Bosque took the reins of Spain in 2008, the nation's football team had won the UEFA European Championship with a team that included Andrés Iniesta, Xavi Hernández, Sergio Ramos and David Silva. Their style and structure was already ingrained, but del Bosque was not afraid of making changes in a bid to evolve the team.

Spain were the favourites to win the tournament, yet they lost their opening match against Switzerland. Rather than change the game plan, del Bosque stood firm and put faith in his players, dealing with the situation with a trademark calmness. By building the team around Sergio Busquets and Xabi Alonso and retaining the short passing and movement of the tiki-taka style of play, they progressed to the final, beating England, Argentina and Germany on the way.

Del Bosque then looked at the devastating potential of the Netherlands and sought to make good use of Jesus Navas' speed on the right wing. The game was forced into extra time, but Iniesta scored in the 116th minute to hand victory to Spain. He then led the team to further European Championship glory two years later.

CARLOS BILARDO
DOC WITH A CURE FOR FAILURE

While it's fair to say that the 1986 World Cup will be forever associated with Diego Maradona, Argentina's victory was actually down to the tactics of the coach, Carlos **Bilardo.** He successfully introduced the 3-5-2 formation – the first time it had been used in a major tournament – and in doing so promoted the virtues of a pragmatic game played to win rather than entertain.

Bilardo was an unusual coach, not least because he was also a trained gynaecologist. Obsessed with tactics and deeply superstitious, he followed his playing career with management spells at Estudiantes, Deportivo Cali and San Lorenzo. He coached the Colombian national team before being appointed Argentina's coach in 1983, and arrived with a reputation for anti-football.

But he was also a grafter, meticulously preparing for games. He nurtured Maradona, appointing him captain, then switched from 4-4-2 to 3-5-2 soon after the 1986 World Cup got underway. This freed Maradona and allowed Jorge Burruchaga and Jorge Valdano to attack, while forcing the rest of the team to remain solid and well-practised.

It wasn't pretty, but it worked. Argentina dispatched England in the quarters, beat Belgium and won 3-2 against West Germany.

○ Schön won 16 of his 25 World Cup matches, drawing five and losing just four

HELMUT SCHÖN
VETERAN OF FOUR WORLD CUPS

Helmut Schön was born in Dresden in 1915, a city that found itself part of Soviet-occupied East Germany after the World War II. Political interference prompted him to flee to the West in 1950, and it was there that he became a true legend.

Schön was appointed manager of West Germany in November 1964. It was Schön's team that faced England in the World Cup final of 1966, forcing the game into extra time, only to suffer the blow of a double-strike by Geoff Hurst to lose 4-2 at Wembley Stadium.

He exacted revenge in the World Cup quarter-final of 1970. Defeat to Italy in the semis, however, saw West Germany console themselves with a third-place finish. Yet in 1972, West Germany became European champions.

There was a sense that Schön would eventually crack the World Cup, and so it came in 1974 with West Germany hosting. Building the team around captain Beckenbauer, they topped the table in the second round and faced the Netherlands in the final, running out 2-1 winners.

He then took West Germany to the final of the European Championship two years later. Yet they were beaten by Czechoslovakia on penalties and, while they qualified as champions for the 1978 World Cup, they lost out in the quarters. It didn't stop him being Germany's most successful national coach.

○ Even though Bilardo won the World Cup in 1986, some called for him to resign over his method of play

○ Italy's 1986 campaign was not as successful as 1982, but Bearzot left his job, having coached Italy for a record 104 games

ENZO BEARZOT
THE MAN WHO BROKE ITALY'S 44-YEAR DROUGHT

Although Enzo Bearzot only had a single cap for Italy as a player, he was determined to make his mark as a manager when he became the joint head coach of his country alongside Fulvio Bernardini in 1975. He soon took over entirely and led the team to three World Cups in 1978, 1982 and 1986, transforming the side from one that prioritised cynical and brutal defending to a group of players that flourished in attack.

In his first tournament, Italy came a respectable fourth and Bearzot, who had been an assistant to Ferruccio Valcareggi four years earlier, was praised for his team's flexible and exciting play. He took the same sense of adventure to the 1982 tournament, although three poorly played draws in Group 1 drew criticism from supporters and saw him impose a media blackout.

The 'silenzio stampa', however, turned out to be a masterstroke. By shielding his players from the press, he worked purely on encouraging the team. They began to play well, beating Argentina and Brazil, knocking out Poland in the semis and seeing off West Germany 3-1 in the final – a first World Cup win since 1938. The move from a highly organised defence to something approaching total football was deemed a success, as was his decision to recall Paolo Rossi after a two-year ban for match fixing. Rossi repaid him with a top-scoring six goals.

"THE MOVE FROM A HIGHLY ORGANISED DEFENCE TO SOMETHING APPROACHING TOTAL FOOTBALL WAS A SUCCESS"

VICENTE FEOLA
THE CONTROVERSIAL WINNER

○ Feola kickstarted Brazil's phenomenal success of five World Cup victories back in 1958

It is perhaps unfair that many Brazilians view Vicente Feola with a tinge of bitterness, focusing less on their country's first World Cup title in 1958 and more on their disastrous performance in 1966. For while he did chalk up just one victory in England (a 2-0 win against Bulgaria), he had the foresight of introducing Pelé – then aged just 17 – in 1958. He scored against Wales in the quarters, put three past France in the semis and two past Sweden in the final. Winning that latter game 5-2 showed how strong Brazil were.

Even so, the stockily built Feola had a reputation for being a little too laid back, and stories emerged of him sleeping on the bench and letting senior players take too much control. He also had a large coaching team consisting of a doctor, fitness coach, team supervisor, psychologist and even a dentist – a novelty at the time. Yet players have since affirmed that Feola was indeed making the decisions, and that he got them enjoying an expansive game. His groundwork paved the way for a second success in 1962, although he was too ill to oversee that one himself.

JOACHIM LÖW
HIS WINNING TEAM HUMBLED BRAZIL ON HOME SOIL

○ Joachim Löw's Germany entered the 2018 World Cup as champions and won all ten of their qualifying matches

Of all of the managers listed here, Joachim Löw is the only one currently coaching a national team. Having made his way into coaching when he broke his shin bone as a player aged 22, he eventually became Germany's manager in 2006, giving him the chance of putting a lifetime of studying the game into good effect at the highest of levels.

Prior to that, Löw had short spells at clubs such as VfB Stuttgart, Fenerbahçe and Tirol Innsbruck. But his initial partnership as assistant coach to Jürgen Klinsmann had seen Germany come third in 2006. Löw repeated that effort in 2010 before finally bagging Germany's fourth World Cup in 2014, beating Argentina 1-0 and inflicting Brazil's worst World Cup defeat (7-1) in the semis before their home crowd, highlighting their confidence and aggression.

As such, Löw is a modern-day legend. His side lifted the FIFA Confederations Cup for the first time in 2017, and they reached the semi-finals of the European Championship the year before. It has meant Germany entered the 2018 World Cup as joint favourites with Brazil, with pundits retaining a faith in Löw's tactical purity and a philosophy that puts the type of player at his disposal above the quality of the footballer.

○ Mário Zagallo adopted a loose starting XI in 1970 that made use of Brazil's finest players

MÁRIO ZAGALLO
THE EVER-PRESENT BRAZILIAN

Mário Zagallo owned the number 10 shirt that Pelé wore in the first half of the 1970 World Cup **final.** He put it up for auction in 2007, but it always held a special memory for him, not least because 1970 was the tournament in which Brazil trod an unbeaten path to a 4-1 victory against Italy. While Zagallo had only been appointed three months earlier, he had just overseen a team that, arguably, was the best to ever grace a World Cup pitch.

But then Zagallo was no stranger to the tournament. He had won the World Cup as a player in 1958 and 1962, which meant, 1966 aside, he'd had a phenomenal run. For 1970, he had switched attacking midfielder Rivellino to the left wing, allowing midfielder Gérson a place and he restored goalkeeper Félix Miélli Venerando. It showed that his tactics were astute, and that his attention to detail was equally acute.

Zagallo still had his clipboard in his hand when he was celebrating Brazil's victory. But what is perhaps just as remarkable is that he led Brazil in more World Cups. A lacklustre 1974 saw the team finish in fourth place (he quit shortly after), while in 1998 in France, he took them all the way to the final, where the hosts beat them 3-0. He was also made caretaker of Brazil in 2002 and coordinator between 2003 and 2006.

Ramsey's decision to play a tight, direct midfield in a 4-4-2 formation ensured England were dubbed the wingless wonders

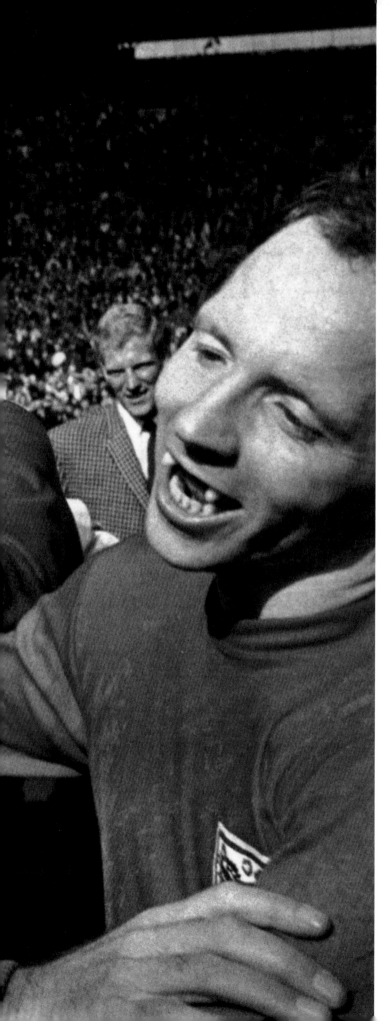

ALF RAMSEY
THE MANAGER WHO BROUGHT FOOTBALL HOME

....

When Alf Ramsey was appointed manager of England on the back of enormous success with Ipswich Town – a team he led from the Third Division to champions of the First Division in the space of seven whirlwind years – he made a bold declaration: "We will win the World Cup."

It was a statement that fans couldn't quite believe that day in October 1962. But it was clear that he wanted to do things his own way. His predecessor, Walter Winterbottom, did not have control over team selections, but that was not Ramsey's style. Indeed, he named Bobby Moore as captain even though the player was just 22 years and 47 days old.

Ramsey didn't start well. His first match was a preliminary round qualifier for the European Nations Cup on 27 February 1963, which England lost 5-2. But England had qualified for the World Cup in 1966 as hosts and Ramsey was keen to capitalise on that home advantage, even though on paper it was clear England were not the best team in the tournament.

He sought to calm his players, even allowing them to watch *Those Magnificent Men In Their Flying Machines* at a local cinema the day before the first game. He treated the side like a club team, and sought to make it as close-knit as possible. This ensured the whole was greater than the sum of its parts and, despite a 0-0 draw with Uruguay, England went all the way.

In doing so, Ramsey proved he was unafraid of making difficult decisions. Striker Jimmy Greaves was injured in the group stage, for instance, allowing Geoff Hurst to take his place in the quarter-final. When Greaves recovered and the press pondered whether he would play in the final, Ramsey stuck with Hurst. It paid off, as Hurst scored a hat-trick to sink West Germany 4-2.

Unfortunately, the momentum did not continue. Ramsey took England to third place in the UEFA European Championship in 1968, but his teams suffered quarter-final defeats at the 1970 World Cup and 1972 Euros. He also failed to qualify for the 1974 World Cup. Yet that 1966 victory for England – which was, in many ways, won against the odds despite Ramsey's optimism – has been enough to make him a true legend for his country. His tactical approach, strictness and demands for high performance won out, and the victory will always be remembered.

ZINEDINE ZIDANE:
A TALE OF TWO FINALS

Zidane went from hero to zero between 1998 and 2006,
highlighting a supreme talent mixed with a fiery temperament

It was 18 June 1998, and France were playing Saudi Arabia in their second game of the first round of the World Cup. They were comfortably 2-0 up thanks to goals by Thierry Henry and David Trezeguet, and Zinedine Zidane was in typically fine form. He was enjoying his second ever World Cup tournament match following the game against South Africa six days before. On that occasion, he received a yellow card in the 75th minute for pulling at Quinton Fortune. This time, however, he would literally see red.

In the 71st minute, Zidane was tackled by the Saudi defender Fuad Amin, who fell to the floor in a tangle of legs. Rather than walk away, Zidane brought his foot down hard on his opponent's body, and the referee, Arturo Brizio Carter, had no hesitation in reaching for his pocket. It was only good fortune for Zidane that France continued to power forward with ten men and bag two more goals to make it 4-0.

As subsequent footage shows, a frustrated Zidane rubbed his face in contemplation as he sat alone in the dressing room. He knew what could so easily have happened following that moment of madness. But had he learned his lesson? France certainly hoped so.

During those first two games, Zidane had displayed the sublime skills that were to become his trademark. He had spun 180 degrees out of a challenge against Saudi Arabia, for instance, to flick a pass to Bixente Lizarazu that ended at the feet of Henry for the opener. It had also been his corner that allowed Christophe Dugarry to open France's account against South Africa. But then it was always abundantly clear that Zidane was an exceptional talent playing in a superb French team. Yet that temper. That temper!

To understand where it may have come from, it's worth delving into Zidane's past. Born in Marseille, France, on

○ Zidane heads France
into the lead against
Brazil during the 1998
World Cup final

23 June 1972 to parents of Algerian descent, Zidane had spent much of his youth kicking a ball around the tower blocks of the bleak modernist council estate in Marseille's tough La Castellane neighbourhood, where many first and second-generation immigrants resided to form a close-knit, life-affirming community.

He'd ended up joining a local football club called US Saint-Henri at the age of ten years old before signing for SO Septèmes-les-Vallons a year later. Duly selected to attend a footballing institute run by the French Football Federation, he was then spotted by AS Cannes in 1986, turning professional three years later. He remained with the club until 1992, when he joined Bordeaux – a great move that saw them win the Intertoto Cup in 1995, but finish runners-up against Bayern Munich in the 1996 UEFA Cup Final, losing 5-1 over two legs.

By then, however, Zidane had already decided to move to Juventus, where he went on to help the team win two league titles, a Supercoppa Italiana, a UEFA Super Cup and an Intercontinental Cup. All of that prepared him well for the 1998 World Cup, and he had clearly shown what he could do. There were sharp glimpses of his internal vision, precise control and immense drive. He also showed an ability to run forward with extraordinary pace, and he was already well on his way to becoming the most complete footballer of his generation, even at that early stage.

Indeed, pundits and fans were constantly amazed that he could find space out of nothing and inspire confidence in those around him simply by being there. They were mesmerised by his mastering of the Marseille Turn, a specialised dribbling skill also employed by Maradona that would see him drag his strong foot back, spin his body and then drag his weaker foot backwards, befuddling opponents.

THE GOLDEN BALL

Prior to the 2006 World Cup final in Berlin, Zinedine Zidane was awarded the prestigious Golden Ball, which is handed out to the best player of the tournament. The then-34 year old had topped a poll of journalists covering the World Cup that summer and, having taken their pick from a list of players collated by the FIFA technical committee, the media gave Zidane 2,012 points – a tally which just edged him ahead of Fabio Cannavaro of Italy, who received 1,977 points. It was way more than the 715 points given to Andrea Pirlo, also of Italy.

What is most likely to have swung it for Zidane – who was not only lacklustre in the opening two group matches, but sent off in the final – were his blistering performances against Spain, Brazil and Portugal in the knock-out rounds. He'd been named man of the match against Brazil, during which he assisted Thierry Henry's deciding goal. Meanwhile, his penalty against Portugal had put France into the final. For Zidane, who was retiring at the end of the tournament, winning this prestigious accolade was an opportunity for glory amid controversy and disappointment.

So to have Zidane out for the next two games in 1998 courtesy of that red card took some of the wind out of France's sails. They may well have triumphed over Denmark and Paraguay without him (they beat Denmark 2-1 and Paraguay 1-0) but, in that latter game at least, they embarrassingly flapped and floundered at times. France needed a sudden death goal against Paraguay courtesy of Laurent Blanc to send them into the quarters. This, however, allowed Zidane to return to the tournament and seize his chance.

Perhaps eager not to put another foot wrong, he was actually relatively subdued in the subsequent stalemate quarter-final against Italy, even though he scored the first penalty in the shootout to help France through 4-3. He wasn't his true pioneering self against Croatia in the semis either but, again, France's overall strength saw them through with a 2-1 win. The victory put France into the final against Brazil, and there was no doubt that France needed Zidane to be at his best. All he needed to do was keep his fiery temperament under control, and everyone knew he would be hugely effective.

So it came: 12 July 1998. The French supporters were heaping much pressure on Zidane's shoulders, their usual enthusiastic shouts of "Zidane" bouncing off the roof of the magnificent Stade de France. By this stage, 'Zizoumania' – as the press called it in reference to Zidane's nickname, Zizou – was in full flow. The French supporters were hopeful that the team could finally lift the trophy for the first time

following the disappointments of 1958, 1982 and 1986, when the country failed to get past the semis.

To get this far had not been without effort and sacrifice. To keep the team focused, they had been staying in hotels far away from their families and this had led them to think only of their single objective: to lift the golden trophy in Paris and become champions of the world. Nerves had begun to jangle as the team stood before the 75,000-strong crowd, but when the whistle blew, Les Bleus showed their intent. Almost immediately, Zidane was displaying his intricate passing and incandescent skills, his confidence raised and a sense of victory already apparent.

If there was any hint that the level of passionate support had weighed heavy on the team and that the demands on the players were high, the players looked determined not to show it. Some pundits had suggested that the immense expectation in France is what had caused Zidane to explode with such force during that game against the Saudis.

One thing's for sure, however: Zidane's temperament improved after he returned, and it was evident in this match. It was his chance to stand alongside the greats of the World Cup, from Pelé to Platini, Cruyff to Maradona – not that Zidane, a man of uncharacteristic humility, would have welcomed the comparisons in reality

Indeed, Zidane was always aware of his roots and, having worked hard, any victory would be entirely earned. He just had to keep the temper and the street-toughness he learned in the 'ghetto' under strict control. The good news was that

Zidane in action during the 1998 World Cup final between Brazil and France. France would defeat Brazil 3-0

○ Zidane takes on Brazilian captain Dunga in the 1998 World Cup final

WHAT DID MATERAZZI SAY?

When Zinedine Zidane was sent off in the final of the 2006 World Cup, it was clear that the Italian defender Marco Materazzi had said something to him. Quite what, however, was the subject of speculation that was only properly cleared up a year later when Materazzi revealed the actual words. It appears Zidane had reacted to having his shirt pulled by Materazzi and told him: "If you want my shirt I will give it to you afterwards." Materazzi revealed to the magazine *TV Sorrisi e Canzoni* that he then replied to the French star: "I prefer the whore that is your sister." This caused Zidane to retaliate.

But does Zidane regret it? Maybe. He admitted to the French sports television programme *Téléfoot* in 2017 that he was ashamed of what happened that day. "I am not proud of this gesture – for all these young people, all these coaches, all these volunteers who make football a different thing," he told them.

Yet, when asked in 2010 if he would say sorry to Materazzi, he was unequivocal. "I'd rather die," he answered, explaining: "If I say 'sorry', I would also be admitting that what he himself did was normal. And for me it was not normal."

he was seemingly more relaxed than he had been at the start of the tournament, when his teammates noticed he was more stretched and demanding.

Easing matters for Zidane was the fact that he wasn't actually the talking point as the game got underway; Brazil's Ronaldo was. About 70 minutes before the kick-off, the footballing press had become rather giddy when they noticed that the man widely considered to be the greatest player at the tournament was not on the team sheet. Journalists spent 40 minutes looking for answers, only to be handed a replacement sheet with Ronaldo in place of Edmundo. An odd state of affairs, it only later became apparent that the striker had suffered a terrible fit while sleeping earlier in the day. Some who witnessed it thought he was dying.

The episode was put down to pressure, which had been too much for the 21 year old. Zidane would have understood. But just as Ronaldo appeared lost and a mere shadow of the player everyone knew him to be, so Zidane put on a masterclass. It therefore became an intriguing final between a country that had won the World Cup four times – the last just four years earlier in 1994 – and a team that seemed to embody the world. That's because France was made up of players with roots in Africa, South America, the Caribbean, Armenia and the Basque country. It was so diverse that Jean-Marie Le Pen, leader of the far-right Front National party, called them "unworthy" to represent France – a disgraceful label and slur against the side that is only likely to have spurred them on further.

And so it was that Zidane had his moment, making entertaining runs that culminated in him scoring two first-half goals: one in the 27th minute when he headed a corner from Emmanuel Petit past goalkeeper Cláudio Taffarel and the other on 45, again from a corner. As the second half got underway, it was becoming ever more clear that Zidane would be man of the match, but France didn't make it easy for themselves.

Marcel Desailly, who was at the heart of the French defence, got a yellow card in the 48th minute and another in the 68th, which led to him being sent off. Down to ten men, it was ripe for a Brazilian comeback but France – and Zidane – remained strong, particularly in their defensive performance and their collective decision to continue to push forward.

Then, in the 90th minute, Emmanuel Petit got on the end of a pass from Patrick Vieira and the game was over. France had won 3-0 and Zidane had become a national hero, his face later projected onto the Arc de Triomphe, complete with the phrase "Zizou on t'aime" ("Zizou, we love you"). In achieving such an upset against the previous tournament's champions, Zidane – who was indeed man of the match – had helped turn France on to the delights of international

○ Mexican referee Arturo Brizio
Carter sends off Zidane for
stamping on the Saudi captain
Fuad Amin in 1998

football after years of apathy. The celebrations continued on the Champs-Élysées long into the night.

Zidane's stock had risen hugely. The following season, he won the Intertoto Cup with Juventus and France picked up the European Championship in 2000. A year later, Zidane signed a four-year deal with Real Madrid worth a then-record £46 million. He was 29 years old, and his immediate goal was to steer the club to a ninth European Cup. Zidane-mania was felt on the streets of Madrid and he picked up the Supercopa de España almost immediately.

By the end of that season, he'd added the Champions League, but internationally, things were less rosy. A thigh injury stopped him from playing in France's opening games in the 2002 World Cup and by the time he came back, in the third group match, it was largely too late and he couldn't prevent his country from being eliminated. Still, back with Madrid, he ended up winning La Liga in the 2002-03 season, while picking up the UEFA Super Cup, Intercontinental Cup and another Supercopa de España. It was some haul in such a small space of time, and Zidane soon found himself preparing for another World Cup.

Germany 2006 was set to be Zidane's last. He'd already announced that he would retire a year earlier, but he was persuaded to give his all for one more World Cup. Some saw him as France's great hope and not just in a footballing sense. Politically, it was hoped he could deflect attention from high unemployment and other such problems back home. To that degree, the pressure was upon him yet again, although the external factors were now wider than football itself, and it could be argued that it was too much for him to take on.

ZIDANE FACTS & FIGURES

3
GOALS SCORED IN WORLD CUP FINAL MATCHES

GAMES PLAYED AT **2002 WORLD CUP**
1

108
OVERALL NUMBER OF APPEARANCES FOR FRANCE

2
NUMBER OF RED CARDS RECEIVED IN WORLD CUP MATCHES

12
MATCHES PLAYED IN WORLD CUPS

2
NUMBER OF APPEARANCES IN THE FIFA ALL-STAR TEAM **(1998, 2006)**

In reality, very few people thought France could win the World Cup this time around, but Zidane vowed to himself to go out with a bang. It's just a shame that it wasn't quite the bang he would have hoped for, as history would bear out.

Just as in the 1998 World Cup, Zidane picked up a yellow card in his opening game against Switzerland, this time in the 72nd minute, which was three short of the previous occasion. France drew 0-0 and went on to play South Korea, hoping to turn things around. Instead, they drew 1-1 and Zidane got yet another caution in the 85th minute. It meant he missed the 2-0 victory over Togo that saw France scrape through to the knockout stage, but in a bid to get the players motivated, he told them: "We live together, we will die together". Things began to get better after that.

France thumped three past Spain to win 3-1 in the Round of 16, with Zidane getting a yellow card in the 91st minute before scoring 60 seconds later. Supporters were overjoyed that the Frenchman seemed to have found his rhythm and he was cajoling his teammates to victory, conjuring images of 1998. Zidane did the same against Brazil in the quarter-finals, which France won 1-0, and his penalty in the 33rd minute of the semi-final against Portugal put his country through to the final.

And so it was that on 9 July 2006, Zidane would play his last game for France before a crowd of 69,000 at the Olympiastadion in Berlin against Italy. Zidane got a penalty in the seventh minute but Materazzi equalised. The game went into extra time and then Zidane seemingly exploded, with ten minutes to go before the whistle blew for penalties. He well and truly lost his head.

After nearly heading France to victory only to see Italy's goalkeeper Gianluigi Buffon take hold, he got involved in an altercation with Materazzi. It had originally been thought that Materazzi had insulted Zidane's mother, but the defender later admitted it was his sister. Either way, it riled Zidane, who initially walked past the player before deciding to turn and walk back to him. With his head down, he butted Materazzi in the chest, prompting him to fall theatrically to the floor. Zidane got a red card and France lost the game on penalties.

Even today, it's a moment that cannot be forgotten – an inglorious ending to an iconic playing career. Pundits believed it may have caused France to lose what would have been their second World Cup title, and Zidane has never argued that it was undeserved. In fact, he has since said his sending off was "a very good thing" because he could not have lived with France becoming world champions if he had stayed on the pitch after what he'd done. It was a noble response from a stunning, albeit flawed, player whose passion for the game could never be questioned. But how different the story could have been.

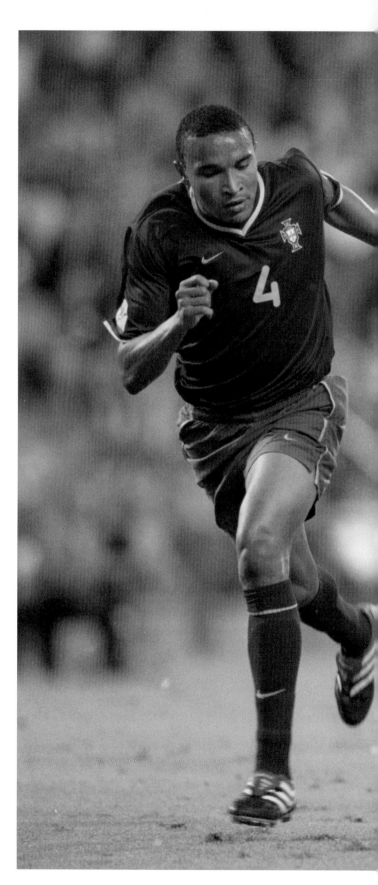

MOMENTS
24 JUNE 1990

RIJKAARD VS VÖLLER

A bitter rivalry spills over to showcase football at its worst

It may surprise England fans to hear that the Germans do not consider them rivals. Aside from the fact that they almost always beat England when it matters, for them, the most important feud is with their neighbours, the Netherlands. That rivalry has led to some explosive encounters over the years, including an infamous incident at the 1990 World Cup during the first round of the knockout stage.

It all started when the Netherlands' Frank Rijkaard was booked for a foul on Germany's Rudi Völler. Rijkaard felt that Völler had deliberately left a leg dangling to win himself the foul and he wasn't pleased, to say the least. Depending on your point of view, Rijkaard may or may not have had a point,

but regardless, that did not excuse what he did next. As the two jogged away, Rijkaard sent a glob of spit into the back of Völler's hair. Words were exchanged and Völler was booked.

From the resulting free kick sent into the box, Völler handballed and then went to ground after colliding with the keeper, despite what looked like a genuine attempt to avoid contact. Rijkaard saw it another way, interpreting the handball and his going to ground as more deliberate cheating. His temper flared again as he ran over to Völler and tried to yank him up by the ear, before stamping on his foot. The referee had had enough and showed both players red. It's exactly what we don't want to see in a World Cup match, but it's a famous moment nonetheless.

TOTAL FOOTBALL AND THE BIRTH OF THE MODERN GAME

Although they came up short, the 1974 Netherlands side is remembered as one of the very best

Which World Cup side is the greatest of them all?

Clearly, a string of wins against the world's best teams is a prerequisite for any candidate, as is an exciting, aesthetically pleasing style of football. The same goes for a healthy smattering of star names, and a classic kit always helps.

What about sides who never actually won the World Cup? Can they be considered too? Devotees of the Netherlands side of the 1974 World Cup would likely say so.

In coach Rinus Michels and captain Johan Cruyff the Oranje of the 1970s were served by two giants of world football. The team will also be remembered for their swaggering, often breathtaking, performances in West Germany over the course of the summer of 1974. They won all but one of six matches in the first two group stages, scoring 14 times and conceding just once.

Argentina, a technically gifted side who went on to win the World Cup four years later, were swatted aside 4-0 in a ruthless display.

Then it was the turn of Brazil, winners of three of the previous four tournaments. Unable to deal with the constant swarm of orange jerseys, the Seleção could count themselves lucky not to have been beaten by a greater margin than 2-0.

Results aside, what made the 1974 Netherlands team exceptional was a set of bold, new tactics. The origins of Total Football, or totaalvoetbal in Dutch, can be traced as far back as Matthias Sindelar's Austrian national team of the 1930s, through River Plate's La Máquina a decade later, and Ferenc Puskás's Hungary of the 1950s. It really took off under Michels at Ajax from 1965 onwards, though.

Given that Total Football is most commonly associated with the free-scoring Ajax and Dutch national sides of the 1970s, as well as Barcelona from the late 1980s onwards, its underlying premise is surprisingly a defensive one. That is, if the opponent does not have the ball, he cannot score. The idea is to make the pitch as small as possible when out of possession. This is done by pushing the defensive line up the pitch to set an aggressive offside trap, while your own attackers press the opponent deep in his own half.

For the Dutch team, this meant quick transitions from a 4-3-3 to a 3-4-3, with the sweeper pushing into midfield, as the situation dictated. As such, the system required players to become adept at playing in more than just one position – a largely alien concept in the 1970s.

Michels' Ajax had used Total Football to devastating effect in the early 1970s, winning four Eredivisie titles, three KNVB Cups and a European Cup, before he exported it to Barcelona. But before the age of satellite TV and online football streaming, it had been witnessed by very few outside Amsterdam and Catalonia.

The watching world was stunned by what the Netherlands were doing, as the World Cup was beamed across the world. Their game differed from that of their opponents so

○ Johan Cruyff under pressure from a West German defender in the 1974 World Cup final

radically, they may as well have been playing an entirely new sport.

Footage from the tournament – available at the click of a button these days – is quite a sight. In match after match, gangs of orange shirts streamed across the pitch in what seemed to be counter-intuitive patterns.

Instead of closing down passing lanes, Michels' men chased after individual opponents, while six or more defenders would sprint in unison towards the halfway line to leave dawdling opponents stranded offside.

While tactical change in football is largely evolutionary rather than revolutionary, it is not reductive to argue that the sport's history can be divided in two by the 1974 World Cup; football before Cruyff and after Cruyff, such has been Total Football's far-reaching and enduring impact. Its fingerprints can be found everywhere in the modern game.

"As a small boy," Arrigo Sacchi, the legendary Milan manager, once said, "I was in love with Honvéd, then Real Madrid, then Brazil, all the great sides. But it was Holland in the 1970s that really took my breath away. It was a mystery to me. The television was too small; I felt like I need to see the whole pitch fully to understand what they were doing and fully to appreciate it."

Today, tactical flexibility and off-the-ball movement are so prevalent that almost all top-level European club sides can be considered exponents of Total Football.

Leaving Ajax for Barcelona, as Michels had done, Cruyff's ideas later became enmeshed in the footballing DNA of what became the modern era's pre-eminent team. The tactical approach of the Spanish national sides that won three consecutive major tournaments can also be traced back to Total Football.

Pep Guardiola, the then-Barcelona manager, who had played under Cruyff, once remarked: "Cruyff built the cathedral. Our job is to maintain and renovate it."

If a team's greatness is at least partly measured by its wider impact on its sport, the 1974 Dutch team can be said to have played some of the most important football of the 20th century.

Of course, football is much more than Xs and Os on a blackboard. The legendary Oranje team was also touched by technical genius and scintillating link-up play between Cruyff and forwards Johnny Rep and Rob Rensenbrink.

Tricky passes, often with the outside of the boot, were employed to great effect, while emboldened attackers introduced tricks and flicks to their game.

The Cruyff turn, in which a player shapes to pass before dragging the ball back behind his standing leg and wheeling

© Like the 1974 team, the Dutch side of 1978 would also come up short in the World Cup final – this time against Argentina

However, as the match wore on, the Germans began to grow into it. It soon became apparent that they had worked with a plan to neutralise the Dutch tactics. Right-back Berti Vogts was charged with dealing with the threat of Cruyff and marking the Netherlands' star players out of the game, while Beckenbauer, Hoeneß and Wolfgang Overath flooded the midfield and took charge of the game.

Paul Breitner levelled the scores from the spot midway through the first half, and Gerd Müller added a second on the stroke of half time. Stifled for the first time in the tournament, Michels' men failed to find another goal, and West Germany were crowned world champions.

They may not have lifted the trophy but the men in orange jerseys nevertheless remain one of the most important football teams ever assembled. Few would argue their status as the greatest team never to win the World Cup.

"Maybe we were the real winners in the end," Cruyff mused, teasingly in 2014, two years before his death. "I think the world remembers our team more."

away, was debuted during the Netherlands' match against Sweden in the 1974 World Cup. Within weeks, players across the world were attempting to imitate the now-famous technique.

The Dutch went into the final against a Franz Beckenbauer-led West Germany as hot favourites, despite playing in front of a partisan crowd in Munich's Olympiastadion. There was also an inevitable whiff of tension around the ground. It was just three decades removed from the Nazi invasion of the Netherlands, the event that has fuelled a decades-long rivalry between the two nations.

The away side made the best possible start; Johan Neeskens converted from the penalty spot after just two minutes following a rash challenge on Cruyff by Uli Hoeneß.

THE ARCHITECT OF MODERN FOOTBALL

As almost every team in Europe's top leagues practises a form of Total Football, it's clear why it is considered the world's most successful philosophy.

Tiki-taka, an evolution of Total Football, underpinned the two pre-eminent sides of the modern era – Pep Guardiola's Barcelona and the Spanish team that won three major tournaments between 2008 and 2012.

It is no exaggeration to argue that Johan Cruyff, who played for Barcelona between 1973 and 1978, and then managed the side from 1988 until 1996, introduced many of the methods that helped it transform into the world's biggest club.

By 1990, Barça had won ten league titles and no European Cups in its history. Since then, it has collected 14 league titles and all five of its European Cups. Much of that is down to the club's enduring footballing philosophy, firmly rooted in Total Football, which remains in place as managers come and go.

The system's success is also evident when one considers that managers with hugely differing styles – from Arsène

Wenger to Ronald Koeman to Marcelo Bielsa – equally consider themselves disciples of Cruyff and Rinus Michels.

Of course, we mustn't forget there are a number of modern sides whose football more closely resembles Catenaccio, a defensive strategy characterised by nullifying an opponent's strengths, which was particularly popular in the 1960s.

But even José Mourinho and Diego Simeone, whose teams have been known to defend very deep at times, ask their players to be able to seamlessly switch positions and rapidly transition from defence to attack – hallmarks of Total Football.

TOP 10: GOALS

You can be the worst striker in history, but score at a World Cup and you're instantly transformed into a national hero

KYLIAN MBAPPÉ VS CROATIA, 2018

⚽ It had been 20 years since France had found World Cup success, but Mbappé's long range strike in the 2018 edition made him the youngest player since Pelé in 1958 to score in a World Cup final. The second half goal propelled his national side to a 4-2 win against Croatia to seal the tournament.

CARLOS ALBERTO VS ITALY, 1970

⚽ In the 1970 final against Italy, Brazil were already 3-1 up when they dribbled out of their own half. Jairzinho found Pelé, a man determined to make a comeback after his 1966 injury, who laid the ball off for Carlos Alberto to thump home perhaps the greatest final goal ever.

ESTEBAN CAMBIASSO VS SERBIA AND MONTENEGRO, 2006

⚽ Argentina manager José Pékerman's philosophy was that consideration in possession, not frantic desperation, would always prevail. Never was that more obvious than when in a single minute, Argentina strung together 25 passes before Cambiasso scored from 12 yards out. The ultimate team goal.

EUSÉBIO VS BRAZIL, 1966

⚽ Some goals echo more for their significance and the players involved than their overall skill. Eusébio, known as the Black Panther, scored nine goals for Portugal at England '66. None resonated more than a half-volley, his second, to seal a 3-1 win over Brazil, knocking out the defending champions.

PELÉ VS SWEDEN, 1958

⚽ Brazil were behind after just four minutes of the final, but a Vavá double put them ahead before half time. Then Pelé produced a moment of magic, flicking the ball back over his defender's head to volley home from 15 yards and all but end the game as a contest.

ROBIN VAN PERSIE
VS SPAIN, 2014

⚽ **The opening game of Group B in 2014 was a re-run of the 2010 final, in which Andrés Iniesta had broken Dutch hearts.** The Netherlands got revenge in Brazil with a 5-1 win, but it was Robin van Persie's salmon-like leap and header from the edge of the box that lives long in the memory.

MICHAEL OWEN
VS ARGENTINA, 1998

⚽ **The 1998 second-round clash between England and Argentina will be best remembered for Diego Simeone getting David Beckham sent off and David Batty's penalty miss.** But 18-year-old Michael Owen had already produced a memorable moment, beating José Chamot and Roberto Ayala in a run from the halfway line to score and give England a 2-1 lead.

SIPHIWE TSHABALALA
VS MEXICO, 2010

⚽ **The 2010 World Cup was destined to be a special one – the very first in Africa.** And while the first half of the opening game of the tournament – South Africa vs Mexico – tested the eardrums with its vuvuzela volume, the second saw Siphiwe Tshabalala emphatically hammer home the first goal ever scored at an African World Cup. Bafana Bafana had announced themselves.

DENNIS BERGKAMP
VS ARGENTINA, 1998

⚽ **With time winding down in the quarter final game against Argentina, extra time looked almost to be a certainty.** However, Bergkamp had other ideas. Frank de Boer played a 60 yard floater to the right hand side of the penalty box, which Bergkamp controlled with a sensational touch, before taking it past Robert Ayala and smashing it past Carlos Roa into the top left hand corner.

MARADONA VS ENGLAND, 1986

⚽ **England were still reeling. Manager Bobby Robson was still remonstrating with anyone who would listen.** Captain Peter Shilton had hardly stopped slapping his arm in protestation at referee Ali Ben Nasser's decision not to blow up. Commentator Barry Davies had only just begun to ascertain that Maradona might have punched – and not headed – the first goal of England's quarter-final against Argentina. But four minutes after the 'Hand of God' had struck, Glenn Hoddle gave the ball away and it was moved to Maradona, some 60 yards from goal. He jinked past Peter Beardsley, turned away from Peter Reid, beat Terry Butcher with sheer speed before utterly bamboozling Terry Fenwick and ghosting past Peter Shilton to score. It took him 11 seconds to score the greatest goal of the tournament.

THE MAGNIFICENT MAGYARS

Charting the rise and fall of football's first revolutionary force

Before Klopp's Gegenpress, Spain's Tiki-taka, Cruyff's Total Football and Italy's Catenaccio, there was Hungary's Golden Team. The Magnificent Magyars dominated world football in the 1950s with a revolutionary approach that would change the game forever. They may not be so well remembered as football's other great tactical innovators, but they were no less influential and deserve to be revered as one of the greatest forces the game has ever seen.

Between 1950 and 1956 Hungary racked up an incredible record, winning 42 games, drawing 7 and losing only one, wowing the globe in the 1954 World Cup, where they scored 27 goals in only 5 games. What made them such a formidable force? A large share of the credit must go to the team's innovative coach, Gusztáv Sebes.

When Sebes took charge of Hungary, football's dominant system was the WM formation, or 3-2-2-3. Sebes took a new approach, implementing a 2-3-3-2. It included a revolutionary innovation: the introduction of the deep-lying centre forward. In an era where defenders were wedded to the idea of man-marking, this could play havoc with the opposition, who would often follow the player into midfield and be drawn out of position.

Sebes also implemented a philosophy that was the precursor to Total Football. He wanted his players to be comfortable playing in all positions, ensuring that the side could attack and defend as a unit and that players had the tactical flexibility to be able to interchange with teammates.

Of course, to play in such a style requires a group of talented players, and Hungary were blessed on that front. The team were led by one of the greatest of all time, Ferenc Puskás, who would go on to have a storied career at Real Madrid and who scored an amazing 84 goals in 85 internationals for Hungary. His strike partner wasn't bad either. Sándor Kocsis had a better than a goal a game average, netting 75 goals in 68 appearances for his nation. Behind that prolific duo was more great talent: the man tasked with filling the deep-lying forward role pioneered by Sebes, Nándor Hidegkuti, and skilful left-winger Zoltán

Hungary legend Ferenc Puskás scores against England in a 7-1 friendly win in 1954

Czibor. Josef Bozsik was another key figure. He would sit deep, using his creativity and technique to play in the attacking talent ahead of him.

If this crop of talent wasn't groundbreaking enough, they also had the 'Black Panther', Gyula Grosics. Grosics is credited with being the first sweeper-keeper, pushing up to help mop up attacks and allow his teammates to push deeper into the opponent's half.

○ The 1954 World Cup final was held in the Wankdorf Stadium and watched by a crowd of 62,000

THE DEMISE OF THE GOLDEN TEAM

The end of the Magnificent Magyars was precipitated by political events at home.
Budapest Honvéd, for whom most of the national team played, were in Spain playing in the European Cup when revolution erupted in Hungary in 1956. The team brought their families out of Hungary and went on a money-raising world tour rather than returning home.

Eventually, some went back, but several key players refused. Kocsis and Czibor, for example, went to play for Barcelona, where both had successful careers. Hungary's star player, Ferenc Puskás, also went to Spain, where he played for Real Madrid for eight seasons, scoring 156 goals in 180 La Liga games. He won La Liga five times in a row between 1961 and 1965, the Spanish Cup once and three European Cups.

With their key players living in exile, the Golden Team was broken apart. In Hungary's next World Cup in 1958 they were eliminated in the group stage.

Hungary's pioneering group of footballing geniuses set off on a phenomenal run. They went into the 1952 Olympic Games on a two-year unbeaten streak, sweeping defending champions Sweden aside in a 6-0 win and defeating Yugoslavia in the final to claim Olympic gold. The team followed up in 1953 by winning the Central European International Cup.

As the 1954 World Cup drew near, Hungary's growing profile led to them being invited to play in a famous match that provided the perfect illustration of how far ahead they were of other teams: a 1953 friendly against England dubbed the 'Match of the Century'.

England displayed a supreme arrogance coming into the game. Though Hungary were ranked number one in the world, the English football establishment and media felt sure that they would squash these European upstarts. After all, England invented football. Add to that the fact that the game was being played at Wembley, where England had only been defeated once, and it seemed certain that this eagerly anticipated spectacle would go in their favour.

It didn't. England were dismantled by Hungary in front of their home fans, losing 6-3 in a defeat that shook English football to the core. England were baffled by Hungary's tactical approach, sent into disarray by their fluid positional interchanging. This was exacerbated by the tendency of England's players to base their decisions on who to mark on the numbers their opponents were wearing, rather than the space they were occupying on the pitch. England centre-half Harry Johnston, for example, was accustomed to marking the opposition's centre-forward, the number nine. However, it was Hidegkuti, Sebes' deep-lying forward, who was wearing that number. Johnston was completely bamboozled by Hidegkuti's approach, unsure as to whether he should be sticking with his man and therefore be drawn out of position, or stay where he was and give Hidegkuti the licence to roam free. In short, England were stuck in the past and, confronted by the future, had no idea what to do.

A matter of weeks before the 1954 World Cup in Switzerland, Hungary reinforced their status as the world's best team in a rematch, thrashing England 7-1. Unbeaten since 1950 and with those two hefty wins under their belt, they were the upcoming tournament's clear favourites.

The 1954 tournament had a unique format. There were four groups of four teams, each with two seeded teams and two unseeded teams. Rather than the round-robin format we are used to, seeded teams would only play unseeded teams, meaning there were only four matches in each group.

Hungary were drawn in group two, along with West Germany, Turkey and South Korea. In their first game, Hungary wiped the floor with South Korea, beating them 9-0 thanks to a hat-trick from Kocsis, braces from Puskás and Palotás and goals from Lantos and Czibor. Their second game

© West Germany's Max Morlock scores his country's first goal in the 1954 World Cup final

○ Hungary and Brazil do battle
in their notoriously violent World
Cup quarter-final clash

was against West Germany, who took the risk of fielding a weakened side. They paid for it, losing 8-3. Kocsis was again on form, scoring four, Puskás and Tóth both grabbed a goal and Hidegkuti nabbed two. The defeat didn't end up being too costly for Germany, who qualified for the knockout stages after beating Turkey in a play-off. Hungary, however, had to go into their quarter-final without their star player, Puskás, who was injured in the match.

Hungary met Brazil in the quarter-final. Given that the two teams had a reputation for playing attractive, attacking football – Hungary on their part having already netted 17 goals in two games – the game was expected to be a spectacle. In a sense it was, but not in the way people had anticipated. The infamous match would go down as one of the most violent ever played, earning it the moniker the 'Battle of Berne'.

Despite heavy rain and a slippery pitch, Hungary continued their impressive attacking form early on. In the fourth minute Hidegkuti came out on top in a goalmouth scramble to put Hungary in front. They quickly struck again, Kocsis scoring a header to put them 2-0 up with only eight minutes gone. Both teams started to commit niggly fouls; though the rain continued to hammer down, the temperature of the game

was rising. One of those fouls resulted in a penalty for Brazil, which they scored, shifting the momentum in their favour for the rest of the half.

Things really got out of hand in the second half when Hungary were awarded a penalty and Brazilian journalists and officials flooded the pitch in protest. Hungary's Lantos scored the penalty, but the incident further fuelled an already ill-tempered game. Six minutes later Brazil's Nilton Santos put a nasty challenge in on Bozsik. The pair traded punches before being dismissed by the referee.

The reckless tackles and bad blood continued as the match degenerated into a maelstrom of incessant fouling and cynical tactics. In among the chaos Brazil pulled one back to bring the score to 3-2. However, all hopes of levelling the match were extinguished with 11 minutes remaining when Brazil had Humberto sent off for a horror tackle on Lóránt. Hungary's Kocsis then struck again in the 88th minute to give Hungary a 4-2 win.

At the final whistle players and officials became embroiled in an almighty brawl that started on the pitch and continued into the dressing rooms to bring a violent game to a violent conclusion.

Hungary's semi-final match would be against defending champions Uruguay. Uruguay had never lost a World Cup match, having won both the tournaments in which they appeared. Hungary went up against this formidable opponent with their star man Puskás still missing. Even so, they took an early lead in the 13th minute through Czibor, a lead they managed to hold until half time.

Within two minutes of the restart Hungary struck again, this time through Hidegkuti. Uruguay didn't give up though. Instead they played their part in making it a thrilling contest, relentlessly attacking the Hungarian defence. Their persistence paid off in the 75th minute when Hohberg found the net, a feat he would repeat in 86th minute to draw the game level at 2-2.

The match went into extra time, where Hungary's superior fitness saw them take control again. Kocsis struck twice to send Hungary through with another 4-2 win, dealing Uruguay their first World Cup loss in an exciting match that can stake a claim as one of the finest in the tournament's history.

Hungary would meet West Germany in the final, with the result seeming like a forgone conclusion. Hungary hadn't been defeated for four years and had just vanquished the current world champions in the semi-final. Their opponents were not even full professionals, having to work second jobs to get by. Add to that the fact that Hungary had already beaten West Germany 8-3 in the group stages and it seemed certain that the Magnificent Magyars would claim the World Cup glory they so obviously deserved.

Despite having not recovered from his injury, Puskás came back into the fold for the final. The decision paid dividends when he bagged the opening goal after six minutes. Czibor followed up only two minutes later, capitalising on a poor backpass. The final was following the script.

However, West Germany quickly struck back. Max Morlock netted from close range in the tenth minute and Rahn scored from a corner in the 19th. Hungary again took the initiative after the equaliser but couldn't find the net and went into the break level.

Hungary kept on attacking after the restart, but a combination of profligacy on their part and sensational goalkeeping on the part of Germany's Turek left them frustrated. Germany's keeper stopped a couple of shots from Puskás and tipped a Kocsis header onto the bar. His compatriot, Kohlmeyer, twice cleared the ball off the line. Then, with six minutes to go, Germany struck.

A high ball into the Hungary box was cleared but dropped to Rahn, who dummied a pass to his centre-forward, ducked into the penalty box and powered a low shot into Hungary's net. The match ended 3-2 to West Germany. Hungary's phenomenal run was over and the defeat would go down in history as one of football's biggest upsets, a match known as the 'Miracle of Berne'.

There were several controversies in the wake of the loss. Some felt Hungary should have been awarded a free kick for a foul on goalkeeper Grosics in the build up to Germany's second goal; Puskás had a goal disallowed in the final minutes of the game; and Kocsis was denied a penalty. There were also allegations about the West Germany side taking performance-enhancing drugs. What made the defeat most painful of all, however, is how much of an aberration it would prove to be. Between its emergence in 1950 and its breaking apart in 1956, this was the only game Hungary's Golden Team lost.

Hungary would never get the World Cup win they deserved. With the coming of the Hungarian Revolution in 1956 the Golden Team were broken up, and the nation would never again reach the same footballing heights. Even so, we should still celebrate the legacy of the team's revolutionary approach to the beautiful game and the legend of its truly incredible players.

HUNGARY FACTS & FIGURES

91%
WIN RATIO FROM JUNE 1950 – FEB 1956

ACHIEVED THE JOINT BIGGEST WORLD CUP VICTORY WITH THEIR **9-0** DEFEAT OF SOUTH KOREA

27 MOST GOALS IN A WORLD CUP TOURNAMENT

MOST CONSECUTIVE GAMES SCORING AT LEAST ONE GOAL
73

STRIKER **SÁNDOR KOCSIS** WAS THE FIRST PLAYER TO SCORE TWO HAT-TRICKS IN A WORLD CUP
2

RONALDO

HOW 'O FENÔMENO' WENT FROM WORLD CUP ZERO TO HERO

Ronaldo never felt worse than after the 1998 final. Four years later, he would have turned it all around

T here is a period of football with which Ronaldo will always be synonymous. In the late 1990s and early 2000s, he was named FIFA World Player of the Year three times. Twice he picked up the Ballon d'Or. One achievement will always rank above the rest, though: his redemptive and emotional World Cup victory in 2002, when he finally helped Brazil back to the top of world football.

However, to fully understand the gravity and enormity of that peak, you must first comprehend the depth of his trough.

Ronaldo had been present at the 1994 World Cup, bookended by two penalty misses: Diana Ross's in the opening ceremony and Roberto Baggio's in the final shootout. The latter had handed Dunga's Brazil their fourth global crown, and Ronaldo had been one of those sprinting onto the field in celebration. But the 17-year-old Cruzeiro striker only featured as an unused substitute in the tournament, and probably felt like he was gatecrashing the victory party. By the time France '98 swung around four years later, he had become the poster boy for Brazil's title defence, and carried the hopes of a nation.

The expectation on a Seleção going into any World Cup cannot be overstated. When Brazil were beaten by Uruguay in a home 1950 World Cup final, three fans present died from heart attacks and one even took his own life. The yellow and green shirts they wear now were only adopted after they abandoned the white ones they had worn on that day. The defeat was a national tragedy. It is still spoken about in hushed, embarrassed voices.

That is the weight that was being born on Ronaldo's 21-year-old shoulders. Now, there was little doubting that in footballing terms, they were more than broad enough to bear them. He had already netted 25 times for his country, and perhaps most impressively 19 of those came outside Brazil. He had moved to PSV Eindhoven after the 1994 World Cup, and after 54 goals in 57 games, been snapped up by Barcelona. It hadn't been plain sailing – he broke the world transfer record for the second time in a year when contract talks broke down at Barça – but he had settled in

well at Inter Milan, and become the best player in the world, as his 1997 Ballon d'Or and FIFA World Player of the Year awards showed.

But he had experienced nothing like being the poster boy for a World Cup. A Cup Winners' Cup final with Barcelona would pale into insignificance. Even the $180 million sponsorship deal he signed with Nike could not match it. The Brazilian team were overflowing with talent and experience, the likes of Roberto Carlos and Rivaldo coming close to challenging Ronaldo for global honours, while Dunga, Cafu and goalkeeper Cláudio Taffarel had all appeared in the 1994 final. But Ronaldo was the jewel in the crown. Everything revolved around him.

The tournament began well for Brazil and for Ronaldo. The Inter striker was his uncontainable self against Scotland, and Ronaldo scored his first World Cup goal in a 3-0 win over Morocco that guaranteed Brazil's top spot in the group. There followed a blip. For the second time in 12 months, Brazil were beaten by Norway, who scored twice in the last seven minutes to put themselves into the second round. "We lost at the right time," Brazil boss Mário Zagallo said. More crucially, they were through to face Chile, whom they had beaten 4-0 a little over 12 months previous, with Ronaldo scoring twice. History nearly repeated itself as Ronaldo scored a penalty that he had won, and added a second 18 minutes from time to seal a 4-1 win.

The wins started to flow: a hard-fought 3-2 win over Denmark, a shootout victory over the Netherlands, and soon Brazil had fulfilled the minimum requirement of their tournament by reaching the final. Anything less would have been an abject failure.

Ronaldo's form was stunning, with four goals and many more moments of magic. There was a chested one-two pass to Cafu against Norway that you'd accuse of showboating if

ONE WORLD CUP TOO FAR

For a man who has scored more goals at a World Cup than all bar one man – his 15 is only beaten by Miroslav Klose's tally of 16 – the 2006 World Cup in Germany was in some ways a bizarre way for Ronaldo to bow out.

Although he was only just approaching 30, the twilight of his career was clearly upon him. The knee injuries from which he had remarkably recovered in 2002 would not go away, and neither would his ever-expanding waistline.

In their final group game, Ronaldo showed flashes of his old self, with a no-

look pass that nearly set up the opener, a headed equaliser and a booming finish from the edge of the box to seal a 4-1 win over Japan. Against Ghana in the last 16 too, he beat the goalkeeper with a vintage stepover – but it was to be his last goal at a World Cup.

When Brazil faced France in the quarter-finals, he was off the pace and lacklustre, only finally testing goalkeeper Fabien Barthez in stoppage time after a sub-par 90 minutes. Overweight and underperforming, it was the last time we would see Ronaldo at the very highest level.

Ronaldo was on top of his game throughout the 2002 World Cup, scoring in every game apart from the quarter-final against England

○ Ronaldo's illness in the 1998 final was seen as a national injustice in Brazil and the beaten finalists were warmly welcomed home

someone did it in five-a-side. There were two more moments, almost carbon-copies of each other, against Denmark and Scotland, where he got the ball out wide of the penalty area with his back to the goal, and the defender assumed he had the situation under control. The ball ended up in the six-yard box inside five seconds.

So more than ever, Ronaldo was pivotal to Brazil's hopes in the final against hosts France, who had in their ranks the only player who could compare to him: Zinedine Zidane.

On the day of the final, an evening kick-off, the Brazilian players went for a customary sleep after lunch. Before Ronaldo's head had even touched the pillow, his roommate, Roberto Carlos, started screaming. 21-year-old Ronaldo was having a fit, frothing at the mouth and convulsing wildly. "I was unconscious for three, four minutes," Ronaldo admitted, years later. "Nobody knows [why]. When you're there, you breathe the competition, everything is about the competition, you cannot disconnect from the competition. It's a lot of pressure."

After the fit, Ronaldo slept soundly, but when he awoke, he was taken to hospital while the rest of the players, all of whom had been disturbed by the shouting and screaming, headed to the stadium, their minds firmly on Ronaldo – and not France.

Just 40 minutes before kick-off, Ronaldo was hastily added

to the team-sheet and he was back to fulfil his destiny. The players later admitted their concerns about whether he was fully fit, and if his performance was anything to go by, he wasn't. Ronaldo lacked the precision and flair that had characterised his tournament, and while defending was not his forte, his allowing Zidane to ghost into the area and head home was indicative of a mental state far from focused.

In the wake of the 3-0 defeat and mysterious goings-on of the afternoon, Brazil launched a full-scale inquiry. Players, coaches and doctors all gave evidence, but the lack of explanation for the fit sparked conspiracy theories galore. Some claimed he had reacted badly to a pain injection to deal with an ongoing knee problem; others that Nike had pressured Brazil to let him play despite not being fit to do so. Only one thing was certain: Ronaldo was flying home without a World Cup winners' medal and would have to wait four long years to right the wrongs.

Fast forward that intervening period, and Brazil could hardly have found themselves in a more contrasting situation to the one that preceded the 1998 World Cup. 'O Fenômeno' – the Italian press coined the nickname and the Brazilians adopted it – tore a knee ligament in April 2000. It had taken the best part of two years to get over it – he did not play a single game for Inter in the 2000-01 season. Without him, Brazil's qualifying campaign had been uninspiring, losing more than two matches in the competition for the first time ever; six out of 18 in all.

Ronaldo did score once ahead of the tournament, a strike in a friendly against Malaysia being his first goal for Brazil in two and a half years.

But he did not even need time to grow into his new knee and new, larger body. Even after so long out, he was no less potent. He scored in every group game, terrorising China, Costa Rica and Turkey, along with Rivaldo and Ronaldinho in a formidable front three.

Just like the 1998 final, Brazil's entire World Cup preparation had been focused around a Ronaldo injury, only this time, it had all come together. The stars seemed, finally, to be aligning. Even England, whose golden generation appeared to be delivering a return to the big time their country had so longed for, fell foul of a sliced Ronaldinho free-kick that freakishly beat David Seaman and secured a semi-final berth against Turkey. There was an element of fortune about that win, too; Ronaldo's shot somehow evading Rü tü Reçber in the Turkish goal, despite its apparent lack of power. The groin injury that had caused him, he claims, to shave part of his head in an effort to deflect attention from the problem, had seemingly faded. Now all they had to do was beat Germany in the final.

But now Brazil also had to take on the nerves and the pressure. Everything that was true four years ago was true now: a nation expected. Hours before the final, unable to ignore the fact that four years ago his world had been turned upside down, Ronaldo was starting to feel nervous again.

"After lunch everyone went for a sleep and to do their stuff,"

he explained. "I was looking for people to talk to – I didn't want to go to sleep! I found Dida, the goalkeeper, and he talked to me the whole time until we left for the stadium. I was very scared."

You wouldn't have known it. Lining up before the anthems, Ronaldo and Ronaldinho can be seen laughing with each other, apparently not out of nerves but genuine enjoyment of the moment. When the football started, their interplay was brilliant. Twice before half-time, they combined to leave Ronaldo one-on-one with Oliver Kahn, but neither time could he beat the keeper. After a third gilt-edged opportunity was blocked, he shook his head with a look that said, 'it's happening again'.

After the break, the balance started to shift, and the German front two of Miroslav Klose and Oliver Neuville came closer to breaking the deadlock. Ronaldo's body language grew worse, but his striker's instinct never left him. After winning the ball back in the opposition half, he followed up Rivaldo's shot and scored a poacher's goal when Kahn spilled it.

If that goal was fortunate, the second was pure quality. Rivaldo dummied over a pass from Kléberson, and Ronaldo's finish was pinpoint accurate. His eighth goal of the World Cup came 11 minutes from time – Germany could not respond. Manager Luiz Felipe Scolari took him off in the last minute so he could receive a mighty standing ovation.

And when the final whistle sounded, where four years ago he had stood lost and alone with the weight of expectation too much for his young shoulders, the flag of Brazil adorned them this time, and his smile was overwhelmingly one of relief. The greatest footballer in the world had won the greatest trophy – and justice had been done.

RONALDO FACTS & FIGURES

SECOND-HIGHEST SCORER IN WORLD CUP HISTORY WITH **15 GOALS**

47 GOALS IN ONE SEASON FOR BARCELONA

62 INTERNATIONAL GOALS IN **98** APPEARANCES

ONLY BRAZILIAN TO WIN TWO **BALLON D'ORS**

TWICE BROKE WORLD TRANSFER RECORD BEFORE HIS 21ST BIRTHDAY

FIFTH FOREIGNER TO SCORE **100** GOALS FOR **REAL MADRID**

TOP 10: KITS

The most vibrant, memorable, and iconic kits sported by the legends and minnows on the world's greatest stage

USA, 1994

⚽ Almost everyone hated the garish away kit the USA team wore on home soil at the 1994 World Cup, at least at first. Who, after all, would want a denim-style football shirt? However, it grew on people and that blue-and-white jersey is now something of a cult classic.

ITALY, 1978

⚽ We had to include one of the kits worn by the team nicknamed after the colour it wears, **the Azzurri.** This classic version from 1978 doesn't overcomplicate things. All you need is that rich blue, a simple badge with the green, white and red of the Italian flag and some white shorts.

DENMARK, 1986

⚽ **Denmark made their World Cup debut with a striking kit design, half thin, red-and-white stripes and half a block of white.** With the chevrons on the sleeves, the black collar and red shorts, there's quite a lot going on, but it works.

CROATIA, 1998

⚽ **Croatia put in a surprisingly impressive showing at their first World Cup in 1998, finishing third, in no small part thanks to the goals of their prolific striker, Davor Šuker.** Their striking chequered red-and-white kit is one of the most memorable in the competition's history.

ARGENTINA, 1986

⚽ Wearing this classic iteration of the blue-and-white striped Argentina jersey, Diego Maradona would lead his country to World Cup glory, defeating West Germany 3-2 in the final. The brilliant yellow of the badge contrasts nicely with the muted blue and white of the shirt.

ZAIRE, 1974

⚽ **The Zaire team of 1974 were not good.** They were beaten 9-0 by Yugoslavia in the group stage and finished bottom with 0 points. Had they got further, this fantastic shirt would surely be better remembered. With a picture of a leopard attacking a football emblazoned on the front, we think it's one of the coolest kits in football history.

ENGLAND, 1966

⚽ **White may be England's traditional colour when it comes to its football kits, but its most iconic shirt is easily the red one that the team wore in the 1966 World Cup final.** Everybody knows that famous image of Bobby Moore lifting the Jules Rimet Trophy high in that very kit. It is proof that the simple ones are sometimes the best: a plain red shirt with the three lions badge on the chest.

NETHERLANDS, 1978

⚽ **The famous kit of the Netherlands national team and the accompanying wall of orange their supporters bring to any tournament they are involved in is one of the great sights of the World Cup.** We've picked out the kit that the team wore on their way to defeat to Argentina in the 1978 World Cup final, with its chunky black badge and sleeve stripes to accompany the classic colour.

WEST GERMANY, 1990

⚽ **It's no coincidence that some of the World Cup's most iconic kits are worn by its most successful teams.** Adding to the traditional plain white of previous kits, West Germany's 1990 version received an injection of colour with these cool angular stripes in the red, yellow and black of the German flag. It was the last kit worn before reunification brought East and West Germany together.

BRAZIL, 1982

⚽ **Is there a more iconic shirt in football than the vibrant yellow worn by the World Cup's most successful nation?** We think not. Brazil's stylish kits have become synonymous with the sumptuous football its teams have delighted us with, and the supreme talent of the incredible players that have worn it over the ages. Indeed, we could have filled this list with beautiful Brazil kits, but we've decided to top it with the best of all. The 1982 World Cup was not Brazil's most successful – it had an unusual two-group format, with Brazil eliminated in the second group phase – but they still treated us to some amazing football, led by legends Zico and Sócrates. The tournament also gave us a stunner of a kit. Brazil's classic yellow shirt was set off by green trim on the sleeves and collar and complemented by those brilliant blue shorts and white socks.

○ Franz Beckenbauer holds the
new World Cup trophy aloft in
1974 as West Germany become
champions for the second time

FRANZ BECKENBAUER
THE ORIGINAL BECKS

The footballer nicknamed 'Der Kaiser' led West Germany
to glory in 1974 in more ways than one

In the summer of 1974, West Germany manager Helmut Schön – the man who had led the team in two previous World Cup campaigns – was clearly at his wit's end. Before him in the heavily guarded training camp in rural Malente was a bunch of players bored out of their minds, fed up with constant supervision, and in open dispute over the bonus payments they should receive if they won the World Cup.

It was that latter point that upset Schön the most. He believed playing for West Germany was an honour, and he was so angry that he even threatened to replace the lot of them with a bunch of reserves. Luckily for the team's star names, it didn't come to that and West Germany went on to lift the trophy. But this apparent miracle was less to do with Schön's mastermind tactics and more to do with the growing influence and talent of one player. Indeed, there is no doubt that 1974 was Franz Beckenbauer's year.

Beckenbauer was West Germany's pioneering defender, and 1974 should always have been his golden chance to shine. The country was hosting the tournament that summer, and it was felt that having a home advantage would ease them over the line just as it had done in previous years for Uruguay, Italy and England. By that point, the Germans had established a fierce footballing reputation. Yet the issues they faced pre-tournament threatened to knock their status as one of the strong favourites.

Still, West Germany and Beckenbauer had learned much over the previous eight years. The defender's calm and composed style of play had been very much in evidence at the 1966 World Cup. There, football fans saw his preference to play the ball on the ground, while glimpsing his equal strength when dealing with balls in the air. He was also a tough tackler, taking games by the scruff of the neck when need be, his passion for victory more than evident.

Certainly, his stature and undoubted skill were why opposing teams would do all they could to nullify him. England midfielder Bobby Charlton spent the 1966 final following him around the pitch at Wembley on what would be a disappointing day for Beckenbauer both personally and as a team (England recorded their famous World Cup-winning victory). Rather than become despondent, however, Beckenbauer went on to revolutionise the game.

Arguably the greatest contribution that Beckenbauer went on to make was single-handedly cementing the role of the attacking sweeper, or the *libero* as it was also known. He believed his club team, Bayern Munich, was too cavalier and he strove to be more efficient. His role would see him 'sweeping up' the ball if an opponent managed to breach the defensive line, and it ensured his play was more fluid. In one fell swoop, he'd transformed a traditional defensive position and become an attacking defender. Such skills proved vital in the World Cup.

The first time anyone saw this at a tournament was in 1970, when West Germany started well, winning their three group matches thanks to a tremendous display by striker Gerd Müller. They went on to exact revenge against England by beating the champions 3-2 after extra time, but they came unstuck against Italy 4-3, again after extra time, in the semis, eventually making do with third place.

Nevertheless, West Germany had become feared. With Beckenbauer appointed captain, they went into the 1972 European Championship in Belgium along with just three other teams: Belgium, the Soviet Union and Hungary. West Germany won not only their two games but the tournament. It was good practice for 1974, but it also came on the back of a lengthy period of domestic success for Beckenbauer, who had excelled throughout his footballing life.

Born in post-war Munich in 1945, Beckenbauer had joined SC München von 1906 aged nine. Five years later, when it became apparent his club was struggling to finance the youth team, he signed for Bayern Munich and made his debut on 6 June 1964 against Stuttgarter Kickers. He went on to establish himself in a strong 1960s side and arguably became Germany's first footballing 'pop star', the original

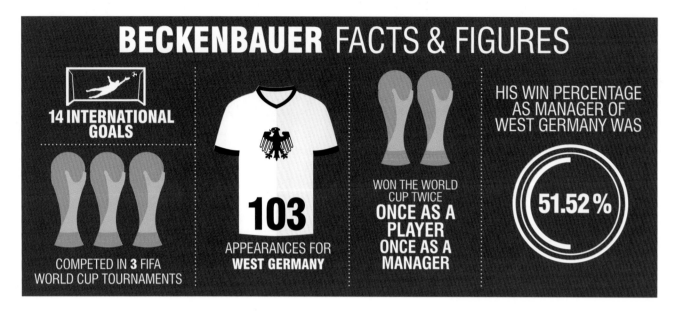

BECKENBAUER FACTS & FIGURES

14 INTERNATIONAL GOALS

COMPETED IN 3 FIFA WORLD CUP TOURNAMENTS

103 APPEARANCES FOR **WEST GERMANY**

WON THE WORLD CUP TWICE **ONCE AS A PLAYER ONCE AS A MANAGER**

HIS WIN PERCENTAGE AS MANAGER OF WEST GERMANY WAS **51.52 %**

Becks so to speak. The trophies also just kept coming.

First was the German Cup in 1966, followed by the European Cup Winners' Cup in 1967. There was another German Cup win in 1968, the year he was made captain of Bayern and crowned 'Der Kaiser' by the *Süddeutsche Zeitung* newspaper. He repaid the faith being put in him during the 1968-69 season, when he helped his team to their first Bundesliga. With 18 wins, ten draws and six losses, Bayern Munich's 46 points put them eight ahead of second-place Alemannia Aachen.

Success continued. In 1974, Bayern Munich had completed the continental double, winning the Bundesliga by a point over Borussia Mönchengladbach and the European Cup in a replay against Atlético Madrid. That was Beckenbauer's fourth league victory and he had also won the German Cup four times by this point. As a major footballing world star and the most important player in the West German team, he also had an agent, a string of adverts behind him and even a hit song. He was at the pinnacle of his career.

Unfortunately for both Beckenbauer and West Germany, however, there was another team receiving plaudits for their talent and play. The Dutch team of 1974 were openly compared to The Beatles thanks to their penchant for playing Total Football and the sheer number of stars in their squad, chief among them Johan Cruyff. Just as with Beckenbauer, there was a worldwide fascination with Cruyff. Maarten de Vos made a film about his life called *Number 14* and he'd won the Ballon d'Or two years running – actually pipping Beckenbauer (the 1972 winner) in 1974.

As such, there was something of a competitive edge between the two players, but Beckenbauer had developed a real knack for being able to proactively read the game. If he lost the ball, he would be able to reactively win it back, no

matter who had it. His spatial awareness was also second to none, and his decision-making was impeccable.

All of these skills would stand him in good stead for the weeks that lay ahead of him in 1974. And so it was that the West Germans beat Chile 1-0 in the opening match before 81,100 fans at the Olympiastadion in West Berlin, and smashed three past Australia at the Volksparkstadion in Hamburg four days later. It wasn't a great performance, however, and Beckenbauer even spat towards the crowd when he was criticised for giving the ball away. "I'm so sorry," he said afterwards, as fans and the press expressed concern that the pre-tournament turmoil was affecting the team's performances on the pitch.

The problem came to a head in a match against a team so very close to home: East Germany. The German Democratic Republic, as it was formally known, had never qualified for the World Cup before, and it was the first time the two countries had met in a professional match since the division of 1949. It was always going to be a troublesome game, politically if nothing else, given the ongoing Cold War. But while West Germany's quality should have outshone their communist neighbours, it just didn't work out that way.

In truth, the game had little impact on either team's progression to the next round. Earlier that same day – 22 June 1974 – Australia had drawn against Chile, so neither German team were in danger of being knocked out. With political tensions high on both sides of the Berlin Wall, however, all eyes were on both sets of players. Schön certainly felt the pressure.

But then there was much to fear. Most of the East German side was made up of FC Magdeburg players – a team that had beaten AC Milan 2-0 in the European Cup Winners' Cup that year. So while the West Germans were, at heart, Bayern Munich, there was some relief that the frustrating first half

Franz Beckenbauer scored twice against Switzerland in his first World Cup tournament match for West Germany in 1966

Despite England's best efforts, West Germany beat them 3-2 in the 1970 World Cup quarter-final

117

○ West Germany
captain Franz
Beckenbauer clatters
into the Dutchman Johan
Neeskens in the 1974
World Cup final

proved inconclusive. It wasn't to last. East German Jürgen Sparwasser got on the end of a long-ball that soared over the head of a pointing Beckenbauer, sped past three fumbling West German defenders and smashed it into the back of the net. East Germany won 1-0 and topped the group.

Schön was flattened to the point where he wouldn't even speak, and the mood became as depressing as the miserable wet weather that had descended upon the country for this tournament. But it proved surprisingly pivotal for Beckenbauer, who virtually held his boss's hand throughout the rest of the tournament, becoming greatly influential. Players would go to him for guidance and they'd urge him to persuade Schön to change his tactics.

Coming second in their group actually worked well for West Germany, since they ended up in a relatively straightforward second group stage. West Germany beat Yugoslavia 2-0, Sweden 4-2 and Poland 1-0 and topped the group, while East Germany struggled against the Netherlands, Argentina and Brazil. Even so, none of the West German performances had really blown the supporters away. In fact, they were unimpressed by the negative approach. To make matters worse, it was very obvious that Schön was having a difficult time, mentally. Beckenbauer attended subsequent press conferences with him and spoke about the tactics and the games. Schön sought Beckenbauer's input and took his ideas on board. Uli Hoeneß was dropped to the bench for the Yugoslavia match on Beckenbauer's suggestion.

As can be imagined, it was a highly unusual state of affairs. Meanwhile, the Netherlands – who stormed through both groups with five victories and just one draw – were impressing everyone with a noticeable swagger on and off the pitch. The two camps were like chalk and cheese but, as Beckenbauer told the German weekly news magazine *Der Spiegel* in 2006, "We took a long time in 1974 to find our feet." Even so, he maintains it was a good side. The fact they ended up in the final against the Netherlands was mighty proof of that.

At stake was the new FIFA World Cup trophy. The Jules Rimet had been retained by Brazil in 1970, and both sides were eager to kickstart the new era. Johan Neeskens smashed home a penalty for the Netherlands after just two minutes and the crowd at the Olympiastadion, Munich, could have been forgiven for thinking West Germany would be overrun. But no. Paul Breitner equalised on 25 minutes for West Germany and Gerd Müller scored in the 43rd minute. Johan Cruyff was booked for arguing with the referee at half time and West Germany held firm.

No matter how hard the Netherlands pressed Beckenbauer, the German's passing remained perfect and he opened up space for his teammates. He was so effective that the Dutch ripped up their pre-planned tactics and sought to minimise Beckenbauer's effectiveness on the ball with strong defending. They let him play in his own half but looked to stop him in theirs, but the deep defending went against everything the Dutch appeared to stand for. The final became synonymous with Beckenbauer instead and the trophy was his at the third time of asking. What's more, it was in the city of his birth.

Beckenbauer retired from international football three years later, in 1977. During that time, he won the European Cup with Bayern Munich two more times and supplemented that with the Intercontinental Cup in 1976. West Germany lost the final of the European Championship in 1976, but Beckenbauer was not only the German Footballer of the Year that year but also the winner once again of the prestigious Ballon d'Or. His legendary status was confirmed.

BECKENBAUER: THE CHAMPION MANAGER

After leaving Bayern Munich in 1977 – the year he retired from international football – Beckenbauer went on to play for the New York Cosmos. He then returned to compete in the Bundesliga with Hamburger SV (for whom he won the title) and had one last spell in the Big Apple before hanging up his football boots.

But of all his roles in the wake of that 1974 World Cup, the one that sticks in everyone's mind is that of manager of the West Germany team. He was handed the managerial reins of his country in 1984, and his impact was certainly swift.

He took West Germany to the 1986 World Cup final, losing only to an Argentina side packing the skills of Diego Maradona. He then went straight to the final in 1990 and, on Italian soil, revenged the previous result by managing his side to a World Cup victory courtesy of an 85th-minute penalty by Andreas Brehme. Even then, having tasted World Cup success both as a player and a manager, his involvement with the greatest tournament on in the world didn't end. He headed the successful bid by Germany to organise the FIFA World Cup in 2006. Unfortunately for him, Germany could only manage third place on that occasion.

MOMENTS

4 JULY 1998

BERGKAMP'S BRILLIANCE

The Dutch master scores one of the World Cup's greatest goals

Dennis Bergkamp has scored no shortage of sensational goals in his career. One of his best was on the global stage that is the World Cup, scored against Argentina in a 1998 quarter-final. Not only was it a fantastic goal in and of itself, but it was scored in the 90th minute to break a 1-1 deadlock and send the Netherlands into the next round at the expense of Argentina. That made an already special goal just a little more special.

The goal is exemplary of Bergkamp's supreme technical skill and footballing intelligence. His first task was to control a raking pass sent from deep inside the Dutch half by Frank de Boer. Stretching for the ball with his right foot while on the run, Bergkamp somehow managed to kill the ball dead. His next task was to beat the defender running alongside him. Bergkamp quickly followed up on his first touch with a delicate flick that brought the ball back inside as he checked his run, taking the defender who had been chasing him out by using his own momentum against him. Bergkamp's third task was to finish. He did it perfectly, stroking the ball with the outside of his foot to send it bending into the far corner. Those three precise touches won the game for the Netherlands and ensured that Bergkamp's name will always be mentioned in the discussion about the greatest World Cup goals.

TOP 10: THE LOWEST POINTS IN WORLD CUP HISTORY

From fascist dictators to organised crime, the beautiful game has seldom shied away from controversy

Part of the World Cup's enduring appeal is its colourful – if at times controversial – history. From Benito Mussolini's intervention as Italy's unofficial kit man in 1938 to the influence of Argentina's ruling military junta on the 1978 tournament, it's clear to see that this showcase event of the world's favourite game has been viewed as a PR event for some.

However, the tournament's most shameful moments aren't reserved for politicians. Within the space of a decade the World Cup has also been the arena in which we have seen mortals like Diego Maradona and Zinedine Zidane rise to god-like status only to be brought back to Earth with a thud.

With eternal glory up for grabs it's surprising that we don't see more players, coaches and administrators behaving dishonourably. Certainly, the integrity of the game has been called into question on numerous occasions over the course of the tournament's history, most notably in 1962, 1978 and 2002.

Beyond such relatively unimportant escapades the World Cup has also brought us moments of true horror, such as the cold-hearted murder of Colombian captain Andrés Escobar, who was gunned down for something as senseless as an own goal.

A low point for people of one country might be another's zenith. Most England fans would tell you the greatest injustice ever done at a World Cup was Maradona's 'Hand of God' goal in 1986. For Argentinians, however, it is something of a point of pride. Some see it as indicative of a style of football rooted in their cultural identity.

Maradona once said, "I like English football. It's just that people go on about the World Cup in 1986 and then I'm seen as the real bad boy. Everybody in Argentina can remember the 'Hand of God' in the 1986 World Cup. Now, in my country, the 'Hand of God' has brought us an Argentinian pope."

Join us as we explore some of the most controversial moments and lowest points in World Cup history.

Italian defender Sandro Salvadore is restrained by Chilean police after the violent clashes

THE BLOODIEST MATCH IN HISTORY
A GAME OF BRUTALITY OVER BEAUTY

A flying kick to the face, a knockout punch and a player being dragged off the pitch by police were just three of the more memorable moments of the group stage meeting between Italy and hosts Chile during the World Cup of 1962. Commonly referred to as the 'Battle of Santiago', it was perhaps the most violent game of football ever played.

David Coleman, the BBC's man in Chile that year, introduced the highlights package to British viewers by describing it as "the most stupid, appalling, disgusting and disgraceful exhibition of football possibly in the history of the game".

It's perhaps worth noting that this was just the bloodiest contest in a particularly violent World Cup. Four players had been sent off in the eight games played at that point, while three legs had been broken and an ankle fractured.

To add to the pre-match tension, the Italians knew it was a game they had to win in front of an Estadio Nacional packed to the rafters. Diplomatic relations between the two countries had also been frayed by a cabal of Italian journalists who disparaged the city of Santiago and Chilean women.

One wrote of Chile's capital that "the phones don't work, taxis are as rare as faithful husbands, a cable to Europe costs an arm and a leg and a letter takes five days to turn up". The reporters involved were soon forced to flee the country.

Ken Aston, the English referee, blew for the first foul after just 12 seconds. Only 12 minutes had gone when the first player to be sent off, Giorgio Ferrini, received his marching orders. Leonel Sánchez, Chile's star player and the son of a professional boxer, then further fanned the flames when he broke the nose of Italy's captain, Humberto Maschio, with a ferocious left hook. Inexplicably, Sánchez was not sent off. He then goaded Italian right-half Mario David into retaliating with a flying kick to the head. David was instantly dismissed.

With a two-man advantage, Chile went ahead through a 73rd minute Jaime Ramírez header and then added a late second through Jorge Toro.

Perhaps spurred on by what he saw that day, Aston would later become the first man to propose the yellow card as a signal to unruly players of the thin ice they trod.

While Italy were eliminated the hosts progressed from the group with West Germany, making it to the semi-final. They were beaten by eventual champions Brazil.

QUESTIONS ASKED AS SOUTH KOREA PROGRESS
THE 2002 WORLD CUP WAS A THOROUGHLY ENTERTAINING (AND TROUBLING) TOURNAMENT

Held in Japan and South Korea, it was the first World Cup to take place in Asia. It was also littered with sparkling football – especially from the wonderfully gifted Brazilian trio of Ronaldo, Rivaldo and Ronaldinho – and enjoyed its share of upsets.

The one serious blemish, however, was what many saw as favourable refereeing for the South Koreans. Few of the country's most die-hard supporters would have expected their team to progress from a group containing Poland, Portugal and the USA, much less make it to the semi-final.

The Italian press have long viewed their team's round of 16 match with South Korea with suspicion, largely due to a surprising number of fouls committed by the hosts that went unpunished.

The game's referee, Ecuadorian Byron Moreno, raised eyebrows in awarding the home side a controversial penalty, which was saved, before showing Francesco Totti a second yellow for diving, despite being a good 40 yards from the action.

Many bemoaned the refereeing in South Korea's following match too. Two perfectly valid goals scored by Spain were ruled out before Guus Hiddink's South Korea prevailed 5-3 on penalties.

However, their luck didn't last much longer. South Korea were eventually beaten 1-0 by Germany in the semi-final thanks to a 75th-minute goal from Michael Ballack.

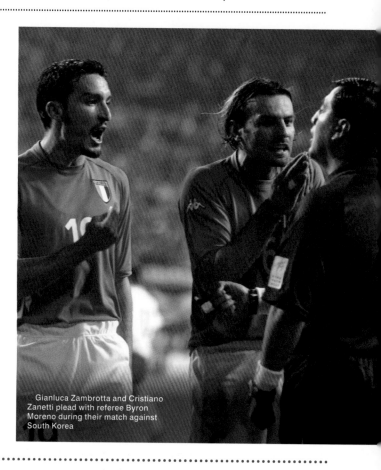

Gianluca Zambrotta and Cristiano Zanetti plead with referee Byron Moreno during their match against South Korea

MARADONA'S WORLD CUP DOPING SHAME
THE BIGGER THEY ARE, THE HARDER THEY FALL

As fabled in Argentina and southern Italy for his on-pitch heroics as he was for his off-field debauchery, Diego Maradona was undoubtedly the most spellbinding footballer of the 1980s.

After a few years in the wilderness with Sevilla and Newell's Old Boys following a 15-month ban for taking cocaine, the 1994 World Cup in the United States was supposed to be 33-year-old Maradona's comeback.

The first two matches, against Greece and Nigeria, yielded two wins for the Argentinians and a goal for their talisman. A sharp one-touch passing move on the edge of Greece's box was finished with a fizzing left-footed shot into the top corner. Maradona was back.

But hours before the final round-robin match, which Argentina would lose 2-0 to Bulgaria, it was announced that Maradona had failed a test for five variants of ephedrine.

The banned substance, if taken in large enough quantities, can be used to boost energy. In his autobiography, Maradona argued that the test result was due to his personal trainer giving him a power drink. Nevertheless, the violation spelled the end of his international career.

○ Diego Maradona reacts after his side score against Greece in their opening match of the 1994 World Cup

WEST GERMANY AND AUSTRIA MAKE A DEAL?
AN UNSPOKEN AGREEMENT SENT BOTH THROUGH

In German they call it the Nichtangriffspakt von Gijón, or the non-aggression pact of Gijón. Algerians, who missed out on the latter stages of Spain's 1982 World Cup as a result of it, call it the Anschluss, in reference to Nazi Germany's annexation of Austria in 1938.

In their final group game, neighbours West Germany and Austria knew that if the former won by fewer than three goals, both would progress to the final 12.

Centre-forward Horst Hrubesch found the net for West Germany in the tenth minute with a keenly taken prod at the near post for what should have been the opening salvo of a great contest. Instead, both sides backed off.

Tackles were few and far between, as were attempts to move the ball into a scoring position. Allegations that a formal discussion between the sides took place have been rejected out of hand. It is more likely West Germany and Austria came to the conclusion independently of each other, although, as *New York Times* reporter George Vecsey said, this would be impossible to prove.

Boos rang out across the stadium, but the teams were undeterred. The match finished 1-0 and West Germany ultimately made it to the final, where justice saw them lose 3-1.

○ West Germany lost 2-1 against Algeria in their opening game of the 1982 World Cup but qualified for the next round with Austria

FRENCH TEAM ON STRIKE IN SOUTH AFRICA
REVOLUTION IN THE RANKS

It's unclear whether the France squad expected much sympathy when they decided to go on strike at the 2010 World Cup in South Africa.

Incredulous that Nicolas Anelka was being sent home for verbally abusing coach Raymond Domenech, the players refused to train two matches into the tournament. Resigning in disgust team director Jean-Louis Valentin described it as "a sickening scandal".

Long-standing resentments over team selection had been brewing for a while, but the catalyst was an argument between captain Patrice Evra and fitness coach Robert Duverne. The entire squad then retreated to their bus, where they drew the curtains and met with Domenech.

In France there was widespread outrage; the squad was admonished by the press and their own government. They were also called to an emergency meeting with Sports Minister Roselyne Bachelot, who reportedly moved some of the younger squad members to tears.

After losing their final match 2-1 against South Africa and finishing bottom of their group, the team was made to face the indignity of flying economy back to France.

In the wake of the scandal Anelka was banned from playing for France for 18 matches, effectively ending his international career. Evra, Franck Ribéry and Jérémy Toulalan were also identified by the Fédération Française de Football as troublemakers, and each received bans.

○ France captain Patrice Evra sits on a bus in South Africa in the wake of a team strike

THE RISE OF ITALIAN FASCISM

AS A RULE OF THUMB, IT'S USUALLY A GOOD IDEA TO KEEP FOOTBALL AND POLITICS SEPARATE

While we all love Sócrates and the Lilian Thuram type, more often than not mixing politics and football ends in a rather public disaster.

The Italian team of 1938, on the orders of dictator Benito Mussolini, managed to offend their French hosts when they lined up for their quarter-final match wearing black shirts – a symbol of the Italian paramilitary.

With tensions brewing across Western Europe (World War II was little more than a year away) it is easy to see why it went down poorly with the overwhelmingly anti-fascist French crowd.

Things soured even further when the Italians – who were supposed to wear white – raised their arms in a pre-match fascist salute, as they had done throughout the tournament so far.

Of the reception they received before their game against Norway, coach Vittorio Pozzo said, "We were met with a solemn and deafening barrage of whistles, insults and remarks. And we raised our hands again, to confirm we had no fear. Having won the battle of intimidation, we played."

The Italians would go on to win the tournament, retaining their trophy, which they would hold onto for 12 years.

"IN HINDSIGHT, WE SHOULD NEVER HAVE PLAYED THAT WORLD CUP. BUT I DIDN'T REALISE. MOST OF US DIDN'T"

THE WORLD CUP THAT ARGENTINA TRIED TO FORGET
A TRIUMPH SEEN AS A TRAGEDY

Daniel Passarella holding the World Cup trophy aloft after Argentina beat the Netherlands 3-1

Argentina's triumph in the 1986 World Cup is the stuff of folklore and is still celebrated to this day. But its other win, as the host in 1978, is seen as one of football's most shameful chapters.

Two years earlier a right-wing junta, headed by General Jorge Rafael Videla, rose to power. It combined the far-reaching persecution of political opponents with state terrorism. Many of the thousands who died under the regime were 'disappeared'; kidnapped and jailed without trial or record. Executions and torture were commonplace.

The tournament was seized upon by the authorities as an opportunity to rally popular support. It has been speculated that matches were fixed, doping was rife and players – both Argentinian and non-Argentinian – were intimidated.

In his book *Death or Glory*, Jon Spurling writes that Argentina striker Leopoldo Luque received a chilling warning from the regime after his side's tight 2-1 win over Hungary. With Italy and France also drawn in Group 1, he was told it was a "group of death, as far as you are concerned".

Luque, who scored four goals during the tournament, later said, "In hindsight, we should never have played that World Cup. With what I know now, I can't say I'm proud of my victory. But I didn't realise; most of us didn't. We just played football."

From the final game of the second group stage Argentina needed to beat Peru by at least four goals to progress to the final at the expense of Brazil. Although it has never been proved, most onlookers today believe the governments of each country colluded to ensure Argentina's passage to the next round.

After trailing 2-0 at half-time, the Peruvians seemed to drop their level of resistance, conceding four more. In 2012, Peruvian senator Genaro Ledesma, who was an opposition leader in 1978, alleged that the match was thrown as part of an agreement that saw 13 Peruvian political prisoners sent to Argentina to be tortured. Others have claimed that Peru instead received a large shipment of grain.

Decades later a caller to a French radio station claimed that the Argentinian players, having been given such a large quantity of amphetamines, could be heard screaming from their changing room after one of their matches.

The final against the Netherlands was a classic. Mario Kempes, the tournament's top scorer, scored the first and another in extra time as the hosts won 3-1. The tournament, however, is best forgotten.

A SICKENING BLOW CASTS A SHADOW
A RUSH OF BLOOD TO SCHUMACHER'S HEAD NEARLY COST BATTISTON HIS

"It was cowardice," West German goalkeeper Harald Schumacher admitted in 2016. "Secretly, I feared (Patrick) Battiston was seriously injured, possibly lying in a coma."

Football fans are not accustomed to seeing dangerous play go unpunished, nor are they used to players being knocked out cold. But in Seville on the night of 8 July 1982, that's exactly what they witnessed.

With the game poised at 1-1 on the hour mark, Battiston, who had been on the field for just ten minutes, found himself running on to a defence-splitting pass by Michel Platini. At the edge of the box he nudged the ball towards goal. It rolled wide.

The onrushing Schumacher, however, only had eyes for the

○ Accompanied by Michel Platini, Patrick Battiston is carried off the pitch in the 1982 World Cup semi-final

Frenchman. Clattering into him at full pace, he knocked Battiston out cold. He lost two teeth, cracked three ribs and fractured a vertebrae.

To the annoyance of the French, Schumacher escaped even a booking. It soured the atmosphere and cast a shadow over what otherwise would have been one of the great World Cup matches.

Such was the animosity felt towards the goalkeeper in France that a newspaper poll found him to be France's greatest enemy – after Hitler.

With the game ending all square at 3-3 in extra time, penalties were required. The West Germans managed to hold their nerve and win the shootout, with Schumacher saving two penalties. However, they were felled by Italy in the final, losing 3-1.

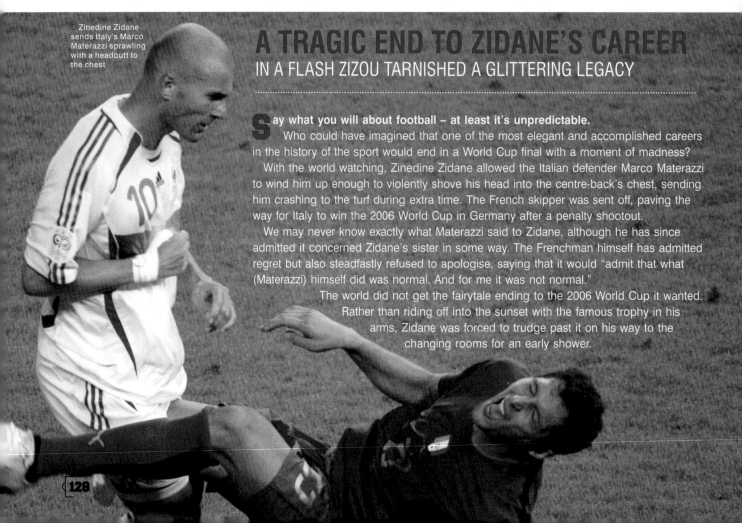

○ Zinedine Zidane sends Italy's Marco Materazzi sprawling with a headbutt to the chest

A TRAGIC END TO ZIDANE'S CAREER
IN A FLASH ZIZOU TARNISHED A GLITTERING LEGACY

Say what you will about football – at least it's unpredictable.

Who could have imagined that one of the most elegant and accomplished careers in the history of the sport would end in a World Cup final with a moment of madness?

With the world watching, Zinedine Zidane allowed the Italian defender Marco Materazzi to wind him up enough to violently shove his head into the centre-back's chest, sending him crashing to the turf during extra time. The French skipper was sent off, paving the way for Italy to win the 2006 World Cup in Germany after a penalty shootout.

We may never know exactly what Materazzi said to Zidane, although he has since admitted it concerned Zidane's sister in some way. The Frenchman himself has admitted regret but also steadfastly refused to apologise, saying that it would "admit that what (Materazzi) himself did was normal. And for me it was not normal."

The world did not get the fairytale ending to the 2006 World Cup it wanted. Rather than riding off into the sunset with the famous trophy in his arms, Zidane was forced to trudge past it on his way to the changing rooms for an early shower.

ANDRES ESCOBAR
1967 - 1994

THE WORLD CUP'S GREATEST TRAGEDY
AN INNOCENT MISTAKE COST COLOMBIA GLORY AND A YOUNG MAN HIS LIFE

The story of Andrés Escobar, which ended with the 27-year-old captain of Colombia dying at the wheel of his car with six bullets in his back, is a tragic and complicated one.

Although never confirmed, it is suspected he was murdered in retaliation for scoring an own goal that helped to eliminate his side from the group stages of the 1994 World Cup.

In the years leading up to the tournament the sport had enjoyed something of a renaissance in the country, fuelled by the cartels. Drug lord Pablo Escobar, who was no relation of Andrés, owned the high-flying Atlético Nacional and paid domestic talent enough to keep them in Colombia.

With a team full of homegrown stars, including Andrés Escobar and René Higuita, the Medellín side won the 1989 Copa Libertadores on penalties having overturned a 2-0 first-leg defeat. Pablo Escobar, to many a Robin Hood folk hero, even nurtured talent by building football pitches throughout the country's slums. However, after the kingpin's death in December 1993 chaos and confusion reigned as warring factions wrestled for control of the region. It was a dangerous time.

If not a pre-tournament favourite, Colombia were certainly tipped as a side to watch in the USA in 1994. They breezed through their qualifying group, conceding just two goals and humiliating Argentina 5-0 in Buenos Aires. Pelé even remarked that Colombia were "the best team", adding that "it doesn't mean they are going to win it, but they will be one of the four semi-finalists."

Sadly for Francisco Maturana's team the pressure soon began to weigh heavily on their shoulders, and they meekly lost their opening game 3-1 to Romania. Worse was to come in the following match against hosts USA, when Colombia suffered the cruellest of mishaps.

A low ball into the box from midfielder John Harkes was met by the outstretched leg of Andrés Escobar. It was a necessary intervention but the ball rolled agonisingly past a wrong-footed Óscar Córdoba in goal. The 2-1 defeat confirmed their exit.

Shortly after returning home to Colombia, Andrés Escobar visited a Medellín bar where an argument broke out. Around 45 minutes later he was dead, having been shot six times in the back. One witness heard someone say, "Thanks for the own goal."

The football player's death has been linked to a number of cartel figures, although the only person to serve time for his killing was Humberto Castro Muñoz. He did 11 years of a 43-year sentence after confessing to the crime, one that serves as a reminder that football is, after all, just a game.

MOMENTS

2 JULY 2010

SUÁREZ SEES RED

Football's arch villain is sent off for saving on the line

uis Suárez is a controversial player. Few deny his talents and the fans of the teams he plays for tend to love him, but his numerous misdemeanours have made him an unpopular figure in the wider football world. There has been biting, diving and alleged racial abuse, but the incident for which he is arguably most famous is his hand ball in the 2010 World Cup quarter-final contested by Uruguay and Ghana.

A hard-fought 1-1 draw meant the two teams had to go into extra time. Deep into the additional period, Ghana's Adiyiah sent a header towards goal that had beaten the keeper. Suárez saved it on the line, blatantly using his hands to prevent a certain goal, and the referee showed him red. The incident probably would have been forgotten had Gyan

not clattered the ensuing penalty off the crossbar, sparking celebrations from Suárez on the sidelines. Uruguay managed to hold on for penalties, where they won, knocking Ghana out of the tournament.

Footballers cheat all the time, but a combination of the blatant nature of Suárez's handball, his ostentatious celebrations, the fact that he had helped eliminate the only African team left in the first African tournament, and the lack of remorse he expressed about the incident – he later called it the save of the tournament and bragged that Maradona's 'Hand of God' now belonged to him – rubbed people up the wrong way. Suárez will never lose the label of 'cheat' thanks to this infamous act.

TOP 10: UPSETS

Reckon a team is a sure-fire winner? Don't bet on it: football can be a funny old game, as these shock results have proved

EAST GERMANY 1 WEST GERMANY 0, 1974

⚽ Packed with footballing superstars and with the World Cup tournament played on their own home turf, West Germany were clear favourites in Hamburg against an East Germany side made up of relatively unknown part-timers. Jürgen Sparwasser scored the only goal in the 77th minute, and the 1,500 East German fans allowed to travel went crazy.

BULGARIA 2 GERMANY 1, 1994

⚽ It was no surprise that mighty Germany – the defending champions who were representing a unified country for the first time since 1938 – would reach the quarter-finals in 1994. But nobody expected rank outsiders Bulgaria to score two goals in two minutes with just 15 minutes to go.

PERU 3 SCOTLAND 1, 1978

⚽ Scotland were Britain's only representatives at the World Cup in Argentina in 1978, and such was the hype around their participation, a stamp was even produced declaring their World Cup win. It was never released. They fell to a shock 3-1 opening defeat against Peru and were ultimately knocked out at the group stage.

SPAIN 0 NORTHERN IRELAND 1, 1982

Northern Ireland had qualified for the World Cup for the ⚽ first time since 1958, and they were playing against the host nation and early favourites, Spain. But even though Mal Donaghy was sent off, leaving Northern Ireland with just ten men for the final 30 minutes, Gerry Armstrong's goal was enough to secure victory.

SENEGAL 1 FRANCE 0, 2002

⚽ Defending champions France had a real stinker of a tournament in 2002, failing to score a single goal and finding themselves bottom of Group A. Former French colony Senegal got the ball of misery rolling in the opening game – their first ever in a World Cup – as Papa Bouba Diop netted from two yards out.

NORTH KOREA 1 ITALY 0, 1966

⚽ With the Korean War still fresh in many minds, North Korea's participation in 1966 was almost scuppered by the British government's reluctance to grant the team visas. But after a bit of to-ing and fro-ing, the secretive side were allowed entry and, thanks to right-winger Pak Doo-ik, they promptly knocked one of the favourites, Italy, out of the tournament.

ARGENTINA 0 CAMEROON 1, 1990

⚽ A Cameroon side largely made up of journeymen from the French lower divisions found themselves up against champions Argentina in the first game of Italia '90. The underdogs went in hard, earning themselves two red cards but successfully neutralising Argentina's star man Diego Maradona. With François Omam-Biyik's 67th minute strike, Cameroon bagged the game's only goal and proved the better side.

USA 1 ENGLAND 0, 1950

⚽ To highlight the gulf between these two sides, the amateur and semi-professional USA team included a postman, a funeral director and a mill-worker. England, meanwhile, had been dubbed the 'Kings of Football'. Yet when the Americans took the lead in the first half, thanks to a goal by Joe Gaetjens in the 38th minute, they held firm. Much-fancied England were humiliated.

BRAZIL 1 URUGUAY 2, 1950

⚽ Thanks to the way the 1950 World Cup was structured (the top teams from four groups entered a league-based final round), Brazil only needed a draw with Uruguay to win, having thrashed Sweden and Spain 7-1 and 6-1 respectively. But although Friaça scored first for Brazil, Juan Alberto Schiaffino and Alcides Ghiggia pooped the party. Uruguay won the tournament.

WEST GERMANY 3 HUNGARY 2, 1954

⚽ Back in 1954, Hungary were known as the Mighty Magyars and between 1950 and 1956, they had suffered just one defeat: this match. Known for their 'Total Football', they had actually smashed West Germany 8-3 just 14 days earlier in their Group Two match on 20 June 1954. But here the two sides were meeting in the final on 4 July and everybody had written the Germans off. Certainly, in the first eight minutes of the game, Hungary successfully proved their might. Led by Ferenc Puskás, who was named the 1954 tournament's best player, they were quickly 2-0 up. But then West Germany hit back in the 10th, 18th and 84th minutes and jaws dropped around the world. The game became known as the Miracle of Berne, while the Hungarian Revolution of 1956 saw a once-great team sadly ripped apart.

David Villa and Sergio Ramos lift the trophy as the Spain team celebrate victory at the 2010 World Cup

SPAIN'S TIKI-TAKA REVOLUTION

Spain winning on a global stage changed the way the game was played forever

We've all been there. You're about to get on a long flight and there's one group of guys who think it's hilarious to have a few too many drinks beforehand, and start doing the conga up and down the aisle even before you've taken off. For a couple of hundred people on the way back from South Africa in 2010, that was the case with 23 young Spanish men. The difference was that they had just won the World Cup. So they were cut a little slack.

The story of that triumph in South Africa goes back years, and features perennial disappointment for a country steeped in football history. Two of the world's greatest teams reside in Spain, with Real Madrid and Barcelona featuring as key players in the story of the game, but on the world stage, Spain had been an extra in the modern era.

After finishing fourth in 1950, they had failed to qualify for four of the next six editions and would not make the knockout stages until 1986 – a run that included winning just one game at their home competition in 1982.

"This cup, this triumph is for all of you, and for the whole Spanish football factory," Spain coach Vicente del Bosque bellowed to a massive crowd in central Madrid – even though at the heart of this most Spanish victory, there was a Dutchman at Barcelona to thank for its inception.

Johan Cruyff is recognised as one of the greatest players

of all time, but it was his eight-year spell as Barcelona manager that left its most permanent mark on the footballing world in the 2010 World Cup.

He engendered his philosophy of possession football and constantly being available for a pass throughout Barcelona and it stuck, so that when Spaniards Xavi and Andrés Iniesta graduated from La Masia, the famous Barça academy, they were fully fledged disciples of the Cruyff way. They had seen his Dream Team win the league four times in a row and wanted to take that success to the biggest stage in the world.

For Xavi, 2010 was his third bite of the cherry; Iniesta, his second. Barça's 2009 Champions League victory with Cruyff apostle Guardiola in charge and Xavi, Iniesta, Gerard Piqué, Carles Puyol, Víctor Valdés and Sergio Busquets all starting the final was a good sign. The 2008 European Championship win and a 35-match unbeaten run that ended in 2009 were very good signs.

And yet within one game, they were in tatters. Their midfield, despite overflowing with talent, could not find a way past Switzerland's Diego Benaglio, and seven minutes into the second half, Manchester City reject Gelson Fernandes scored one of the great scrappy goals after it pinballed off two Spanish defenders and Iker Casillas.

Spain had 22 shots on goal, a stat they nearly matched in their second group game against Honduras – but on that occasion, their 19 efforts did at least herald two goals, even if profligacy was a running theme. David Villa grabbed them both.

"He has scored whenever he wants," Del Bosque would say ahead of the semi-final. That wasn't quite true. He should have scored at least four against Honduras, missing from the spot. Perfection was still a distance away.

The final group game had plenty riding on it, with the runner-up in Group H facing Brazil in the second round. It was a keen sword of Damocles to hang over a game between two sides who knew each other well, and Marcelo Bielsa's Chile seemed unlikely to roll over without a fight.

But for once, luck was on Spain's side. A goalkeeping blunder and a controversial red card for Chile's Marco Estrada helped them secure a 2-1 win, and Spain were through.

It set up their sternest test yet: a clash with Cristiano Ronaldo's Portugal. And the goal that put the Real Madrid star out was Barcelona through and through. Iniesta played a delicate pass between two defenders into Xavi's feet, who flicked the ball off the outside of his foot into the path of Villa who, with an hour gone, produced a familiar and decisive finish.

The same scoreline – 1-0 Spain, Villa – saw them dispatch Paraguay to move into the last four. On paper, Spain weren't vintage; Villa's winner coming seven minutes from the end. They were winning while not thrashing sides, but one flash of brilliance every 90 minutes was proving enough. Just.

It is not the sort of form in which you want to find yourselves against World Cup semi-final regulars Germany. They had put four past England and Argentina in the previous rounds and were the exciting team of the tournament. But Spain just kept winning 1-0, doing so for the third time in a row to reach a first-ever final.

The fact was that Spain were keeping the ball so much that sides were left with precious little opportunity to score for themselves. Against Germany, Spain had 61 per cent possession. Against Paraguay, 62. In defeat to Switzerland, it was 67. It was the Barcelona-Cruyff training in action: be available, want the ball, keep the ball. No one passed the ball more than Xavi, Xabi Alonso and Sergio Busquets in the 2010 World Cup. If you have the ball, the other team can't score.

And had Spain's finishing been even a little better, the story of the 2010 World Cup might have been an even more dominant one. The 1-0 wins on paper may appear meagre, but in fact, Spain's quality was so high that a narrow win was the floor rather than the ceiling of their performance.

But it required an immense level of quality from every player to do so, and attacking players who could unpick defences

○ Xabi Alonso of Spain (left) is fouled by Nigel de Jong of the Netherlands

from settled positions, where disciplined defenders would not be pulled around.

It seemed fitting that a style based so much around playing the perfect game of football – where the winning side would keep the ball at all times – would come up against one that was ultimately pragmatic in the final.

Just as José Mourinho's Inter Milan midfield of Esteban Cambiasso and Thiago Motta had won the Champions League that year, so the Netherlands had Mark van Bommel and Nigel de Jong.

The Dutch side tried to impose themselves physically on the relatively diminutive Spaniards. One of the abiding memories of the final was de Jong kicking Alonso in the chest, but failing to be shown the red card. English referee Howard Webb regards that game, in which he was forced to show 14 yellow cards and one red, as one of the toughest of his life.

Soccer City and its 84,490 fans were in the end treated, as they often had been by Spain, to just one moment of real quality. And it was fitting that it was Iniesta who produced it. Found by fellow La Masia graduate Cesc Fàbregas in the box, he hit a bouncing ball into the far corner with just four minutes of extra time remaining. Spain were spared penalties, their enemy before and during the 2010 World Cup, and history beckoned them with open arms.

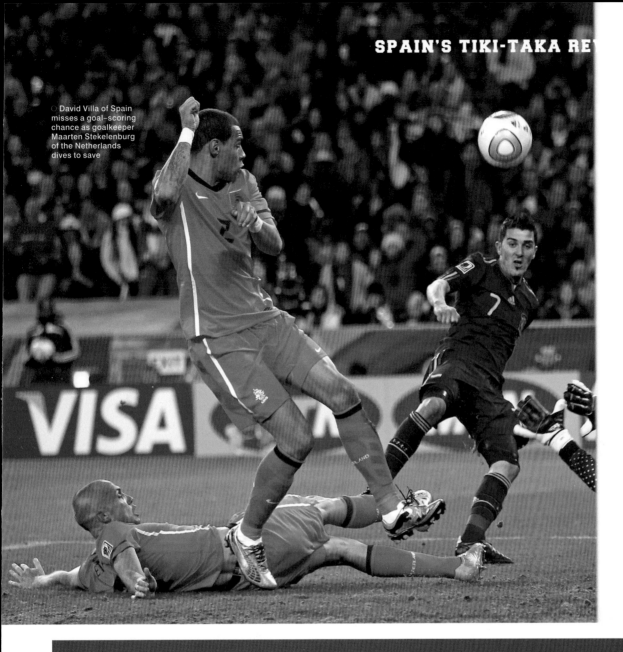

○ David Villa of Spain misses a goal-scoring chance as goalkeeper Maarten Stekelenburg of the Netherlands dives to save

JOHAN CRUYFF, THE FATHER OF TIKI-TAKA

As a player at Barcelona, Cruyff won La Liga, the Ballon d'Or and was the Golden Ball winner of 1974. But it is as a coach that the Spaniards of the 21st century came to know his name so prominently. "Nothing in football would be possible without the arrival and the unequalled charisma and talent of Johan Cruyff," Pep Guardiola has said.

When Cruyff took over as Barcelona boss, already a league winner there as a player, they had finished sixth in the league the year before and won La Liga just once in 15 years. It is a testament to his success that he left eight years later having championed Spain four times and Europe once.

But equally, his revolution was not an instant or an obvious one. "I'm never afraid of making mistakes and I tried to bring that idea to the pitch," Cruyff said. "I told players not to be afraid: 'If you have an idea, good: try it. And if it goes wrong, don't worry.'"

His ideology was a simple one: that football should be studied, analysed and played in an innovative and attacking way, with every player on the field contributing to keeping the ball. No player at the club, top to bottom, was exempt from his revolution.

"If we want things to change, we must change history," he said on his arrival as manager. He would shape the future too, at Barcelona and all over Spain.

TOP 10: FUTURE LEGENDS

Who are the next generation of World Cup legends? We try to predict the future

PHIL FODEN

There are only a handful of players that are able to light up a football pitch with their exuberant style of play and a smaller number still have been English. Phil Foden looks to be a rising star both for Manchester City at the club level, where he has impressed among scores of other footballing stars, but also for England in the next World Cup.

MARCO ASENSIO

With his ability to score goals from midfield and create chances for his teammates, Real Madrid's Marco Asensio is Spanish football's great hope for the future. He and club mate Isco are seen by many in Spain as long-term successors to Andrés Iniesta and Xavi, the linchpins of Spain's 2010 World Cup-winning team.

LEROY SANÉ

With such a wealth of talent at their disposal, Sané is yet to truly establish himself for the German national team despite playing a starring role for Manchester City as they stormed to the Premier League title in 2017-18. He made his international debut for Germany in 2015 against France but was surprisingly dropped for the 2018 World Cup. Germany sorely missed him.

YOURI TIELEMANS

Another product of Belgium's golden generation, creative midfielder Tielemans is considered one of the hottest prospects in world football. He began his career at Anderlecht, winning two league titles before moving to Monaco. Now on loan at Leicester City, he made his Belgium debut in 2016 and played four times at the 2018 World Cup as Belgium finished third.

PAULO DYBALA

Dybala has formed a formidable partnership with compatriot Gonzalo Higuaín for Italian giants Juventus, but he's yet to make his mark for the Argentinian national side. With Lionel Messi coming to the end of his illustrious career, could Dybala go one better than his countryman and win Argentina their first World Cup since 1986?

MARCUS RASHFORD

⚽ Rashford was selected in England's Euro 2016 squad less than four months after making his debut for his club side, Manchester United. In the lead-up to the tournament he became the youngest Englishman to score on his international debut after finding the net against Australia. Making two appearances in a disappointing Euros campaign, he only featured briefly at the 2018 World Cup. Even so, he looks set for a bright future.

TIMO WERNER

⚽ With the World Cup's all-time leading goalscorer Miroslav Klose retiring after the 2014 World Cup, Werner has big boots to fill for Germany, something the RB Leipzig striker is capable of doing. Linked with a string of top European clubs, Werner has been in prolific form since joining the Bundesliga side in 2016 and scored seven goals in his first 12 appearances for Germany. Can he surpass his countryman? Only time will tell, but if Germany are to put last summer's World Cup nightmare behind them they will need Werner to continue his fine form.

BUKAYO SAKA

⚽ Despite falling short in the 2020 Euros final against Italy, the 20-year-old surely has a bright future ahead of him with the English national side. He is known for his attacking incisiveness and creativity, helping to carve up defences for both Arsenal at the club level, as well as contributing to England's recent run of form on the international stage.

GIANLUIGI DONNARUMMA

⚽ Racking up over 200 appearances for AC Milan and 33 appearances for the Italian national team at the age of only 22, Gianluigi Donnarumma is set for a bright future at the World Cup. Donnarumma caught the world's attention with his incredible performance during the 2020 Euros, where he kept his cool during the penalty shoot-out against England in the final to secure the win for Italy.

GABRIEL JESUS

⚽ In Brazil they have high hopes for Gabriel Jesus. "He's the new Ronaldo," claimed Daniel Alves in 2017. "They have similar qualities, a similar drive. He's going to be one of the greats." Could Jesus really be the second coming of 'O Fenômeno'?

After making his name at Palmeiras in Brazil, the striker moved to England in 2017 to join Pep Guardiola's revolution at Manchester City, becoming one of the shining lights in world football in the process. He soon became a vital part of the team, taking the starting place of prolific Argentinian striker and the club's all-time leading scorer Sergio Agüero and helping Manchester City win the Premier League in 2017-18.

His international debut for Brazil came in September 2016, with Jesus scoring twice in a 3-0 win over Ecuador. Since then he's been a regular fixture in the side. Whether his name will be as synonymous with the World Cup as Ronaldo, however, remains to be seen.

MOMENTS
8 JULY 2014

KILLING THE DREAM

Germany send Brazil crashing out of the World Cup with a 7-1 thrashing

Brazil weren't in an ideal state coming into their semi-final match against Germany in the 2014 World Cup. Their star player, Neymar, had been injured in the previous game against Colombia and captain Thiago Silva was suspended. Still, Brazil were going into the match undefeated and were playing on home soil. It was expected to be a close game.

What followed was a humiliation dubbed the *Mineirazo*, a reference to Brazil's shock defeat in the 1950 World Cup final, also played on home soil, known as the *Maracanazo*. Brazil were a mess and were comfortably dismantled by a German team, who would go on to win the tournament.

Müller struck first, converting from a corner after he was allowed to go unmarked in the box. Then, in an incredible six minutes, Brazil collapsed as Germany netted four goals to destroy their World Cup hopes. Klose scored in the 23rd minute to take his total World Cup tally to 16, overtaking the all-time top-scorer record held by Brazil's Ronaldo. Kroos then drilled one in with his left from the edge of the box in the 24th minute and slotted a tap-in home in the 26th. Khedira popped up to give Germany a 5-0 lead in the 29th minute that they took into the half-time break. Schürrle came on in the second half to net another two, the second a thunderous strike into the near top corner. Brazil could only grab a consolation in the 90th minute through Oscar to bring an embarrassing, but entertaining, 7-1 defeat to a close.